Praise for *Changing G*

"Riding across America is about so much more than covering a few thousand miles by bike. Leah Day writes about her adventures, both internal and on the road, with insight and empathy, bringing readers along for a view of magic moments, big and small."

—Alex Strickland, editor of *Adventure Cyclist* magazine

"Leah is not only brave enough to bike across the country with her teenage son, Oakley, but to bring us all along on the journey through her writing—it's open, honest, and completely hilarious at times. Leah reminds us that adventures are not just about the places we go, but about relationships, accepting challenges, and continuing to grow up no matter our age."

—Ainsley Judge, manager of Portland Gear Hub

"It is because of—not in spite of—the dog chases, wrong turns, soggy ramen, mechanical breakdowns, and rainy climbs that Leah and Oakley's trip is a success. *Changing Gears* reminds us that without challenge, we can't change."

—Sara Dykman, author of *Bicycling with Butterflies* and founder of beyondabook.org

CHANGING
GEARS

Published by Familius LLC, www.familius.com
PO Box 1249, Reedley, CA 93654

Familius books are available at special discounts for bulk purchases, whether
for sales promotions or for family or corporate use. For more information,
contact Familius Sales at orders@familius.com.

Library of Congress Control Number: 2022932440

Print ISBN 9781641706544
Ebook ISBN 9781641706681

Printed in the United States of America

Edited by Michele Robbins, Tina Hawley, and Sarah Echard
Cover design by Carlos Guerrero
Book design by Maggie Wickes

10 9 8 7 6 5 4 3 2 1

First Edition

CHANGING
GEARS

A Distant Teen, a Desperate Mother,
and 4,329 Miles Across the
TransAmerica Bicycle Trail

LEAH DAY

To Finn, Jonah, Raven, and
Oakley. Thank you for all the
adventures and all the forgiveness.

Contents

Introduction

It is all about expanding and contracting. Everything does it. In and out, then in again. From small to large to small. From seed to flower to seed. The speck of an egg swelling to rounded middle age and then reduced to a speck of dust. The Universe, for God's sake. Sound. Everything. It all comes and goes, grows and shrinks, and we dance between it all.

When Oakley and I pedaled across the United States, the world was big and bright, and the land was laid out before us, calling and limitless. The sun softened our backs and turned the prairie grasses golden and red. The mountains reached up into the sky, often spiking up through the clouds. The waters of the rivers were startingly cold, the midday heat oppressively hot, making us run for shelter. Canyons were tight and maze-like, and farm fields extended beyond the horizon. People opened homes, churches, fire stations, and city parks with welcoming warmth.

"Come in," they said.

"Rest."

"You are safe here."

The world was like an open flower.

In 2020 the coronavirus caused that flower to contract. It was time to stay closer to home and shrink our social circles until the pandemic passed.

On good days, I could understand that there was beauty in this. As Walt Whitman says in *Leaves of Grass*, "The narrowest hinge in my hand puts to scorn all machinery." It seemed the time to find adventure in the little things and to be amazed by the everyday. I admit that it was hard for me and for Oakley. We are thrill seekers and struggle with focus and stillness but, nonetheless, I have found that with all this quiet it was easier to look inward. And when I did, I saw that I am not just full of blood and guts, but full of all the adventures I have had and the people I have known and the beauty I have seen. It is still there, right beneath the skin.

In our story you will hear the crickets in Idaho, which were as big as our thumbs and covered the road in a feeding frenzy, cannibalizing each other, jumping up against our legs, and crunching under our tires as we careened down hills and mountain passes.

You will feel what it is like to bed down under and beside fire trucks on scrubbed-clean cement floors while reading out loud and being read to, filled with delight to be safe from the cold rain thundering outside because of the trust that a small town had in us to stay unwatched with their millions of dollars of equipment.

You will understand what it was like to hide from the wind behind the scarce buildings on the Colorado plains while eating Pringles and cheese sticks, so tired and sweaty that we could not speak as we slowly notice prairie dog noses popping up out of holes all around. One barked, and then another. Then they turned into a bunch of chatter-boxes, spreading the news that there were two sweating cyclists sitting right smack in their yard. And still we just sat.

And you may feel the tautness of a relationship between a mother and a teenage son that is full of challenge and reward, frustration and love, and a growing bond that will hopefully help us navigate the way through much more than a bike ride.

I know everything will open up again and that there are endless adventures ahead of us—all of us.

This contraction will expand. Until then, join us.

Devil or Angel

October 20, 2019

Mallard Duck Campground, Virginia

There is a deluge of rain hammering on the roof of the picnicking pavilion. My son and I are feeling grateful for the added cover over our tent on this rainy night. We are camping on the western flanks of the Appalachian Mountains at the Mallard Duck Campground. The water is beginning to seep across the concrete floor and pool, lazily snaking its way ever closer to our temporary home. Sixteen-year-old Oakley sleeps beside me, blissfully unaware.

Dear God, I think to myself, *I need to put on my cheerleading hat for this one.*

Today is what some TransAmerica cyclists have called our last big challenge. We need to climb Mount Vesuvius, a steep four-mile ascent of 3,500 feet. Then we will follow the Blue Ridge Parkway for thirty-five miles and descend out of the mountains and on toward the coast of Virginia.

I sneak out of the tent and rustle up some coffee, hoping it will help me put on my happy face before Oakley stirs. The rain is coming down in torrents. We have been riding for nearly three months, all the way from Astoria, Oregon, and have traveled over four thousand miles. We have been camping most the way in all sorts of weather, and needless to say, I am losing my tolerance for wet mornings.

After two strong cups of coffee, I am ready to try my best to put a shine on the day, and I wake Oakley up with a promise of hot chocolate. He takes one look around and lies back down. "You have got to be kidding me," he mutters. But he sees that there is no choice. The island of dry that our tent is perched on has shrunk to a mere footprint, and it is time to pack it up.

1

We persevere through a gloppy breakfast of apple-spice instant oatmeal and stow our gear in the trash bags that line our panniers. We dawdle a little, wishing the rain would let up a bit, but it doesn't seem to be cooperating, so we suit up in our rain pants and jackets and try to enjoy one last moment of having dry toes.

"Okay, Oakley, it's time."

Suddenly, like a Hail Mary, a pickup truck comes barreling across the lawn, sloshing through lake-sized puddles, and pulls up beside us. The driver is the owner of the campground.

"You all are crazy," he shouts over the din of the storm. "Put those bicycles in my truck, and I'll drive you up that mountain. Nobody should be biking up there in this." He climbs out of his truck and runs over to our little shelter. "Listen, I done took eight bikers up this hill before. It isn't anything to be ashamed of. Come on."

The rain seems to intensify as if on cue. It would be so nice to get a ride. I am so exhausted, and another wet ride up to a cold ridgeline sounds torturous.

"Thanks, but we can't," I say. "That would be cheating."

"Come on now. It's not cheating. Your bikes would still be going up that mountain, and look at your son." I look at Oakley. His eyes are bright with hope. He is positively taut with it.

"Mom, come on. It's awful out there. Please. No one will know." I hesitate. It is so cold and wet. "Please," he begs.

In that moment I waver. I am no Odysseus on a heroic quest. I am much more like Bilbo Baggins in The Hobbit, a reluctant adventurer. I would like to stay dry. We have crossed the high deserts of Oregon, climbed the continental divide eight times, raced through the hollows of Kentucky with wild dogs at our heels, and fought our way through the winds of Kansas—and now I am just plain tired.

"This man wants to help us; it would make him feel good," whispers Oakley.

A battle rages inside me. Is the campground owner the devil or an angel? I feel myself waffle.

Then Oakley puts on his bike helmet, and I realize he is expecting me to say no. He needs me to say no. He is unintentionally leading me and by so doing has made up my mind.

"Thank you so much," I tell the man, "but we have to do this."

"You all are crazy," the man mutters as we saddle up and head out into the wet, cold morning.

Maybe we are. Within minutes my sneakers have become sponges, my gloves are sodden, and my bangs are plastered to my head. I look at Oakley and see rain dripping from the tip of his nose.

The climb is punishing. The road's switchbacks rise up and up and up through the dense Virginian forest, one hairpin turn after another. Several times I question what the chances are of a fifty-year-old woman having a heart attack. After an hour, Oakley and I finally make it to the top. We are cold and wet, but the last climb is behind us. Triumphant, we stand together gasping for breath. While we lean over our handlebars, I meet his eyes and can't help but ask, "Do you wish we had gotten that ride?"

"Yes!" he answers. But now he is grinning from ear to ear, and I grin back. What a stinking liar. I would say we both play our roles very well.

Following His Lead

January 15, 2019

Portland, Maine

Sometimes I feel like I live in this van, right here on this grimy uphol-stered seat amidst a patina of dog hair, food crumbs, coffee stains, and unidentifiable sandy grit. Today I am waiting in the parking lot of the Portland YMCA to pick up Oakley from swim team practice on a dark, rainy November evening. Because the weather is so gross, I am surprising him with a ride rather than his expected walk through town to the ferry terminal.

The clock on the dash reads 7:15. I am plenty early, and I have a few minutes before he should come strolling out of the building. The wipers sweep incessantly across the windshield, and the car radio drones on, playing a song that I have heard far too many times. The DJ repeats the station's tagline: "Different is good." It's so irritating I could scream. Nothing different here. I feel restless, on edge.

It's now 7:20, and a slight premonition begins to prickle my skin. I ignore it and take out my phone. Nobody has texted me; no new emails either. How about some Candy Crush? Level 254.

By day I run a private practice counseling service. It is a good gig, and business is booming, but sometimes I feel like a fraud. My whole therapeutic approach boils down to the following: Follow your values, commit to actions that support them, and you can get through anything.

Level 254? What a waste.

7:25—That prickly sensation has grown. It is morphing into a thought. Here I sit, waiting. For what?

7:30—Suddenly, I am sure that I am waiting for nothing. Oakley is not in the YMCA. I know this as sure as I know that the sun has set.

He isn't late yet, but I am certain. I have a spot-on intuition borne from years of experience. I know this kid and all his tricks. Why would I ever think he is where he said he would be? Without another moment's hesitation, I pull out of the drop-off/pick-up spot and onto the road. Commuter traffic clogs the way, and the radio and wipers begin to rattle me. Where is Oakley? I have lost him again. Ugh!

This is the story of our life together. He runs, and I chase him. As I make my way through town to the ferry terminal where Oakley will eventually end up catching the boat home, I am feeling bitter and exhausted. I think of Prometheus and how he was chained to a rock on the top of a mountain, where an eagle would come to eat his liver every day. Due to Prometheus's immortality, the liver would always grow back so he would not die, but the eagle returned every day to do it again and again. Am I Prometheus or the eagle?

7:35—I finally make it to the ferry terminal, but I don't see Oakley through the glass walls of the brightly lit waiting room. The boat doesn't leave for nearly forty-five minutes. Oakley shouldn't be here yet; he should still be in that pool. I feel a rising anger. The little brat. I should have known to never let my guard down. He never went to swim practice. He has been lying to me all week, I am sure. Where has he been? Fury begins to boil inside me.

7:40—From my seat in the van, I peer out into the darkness, searching for him. The docks are cold and wet, and the wind is blowing off the ocean. I am torn between wanting and not wanting to find him here. It doesn't take long. There he is, standing out on the city pier in the rain, hood up, sneakers scuffing at the pavement, down jacket soaked through. He looks miserable. What is he doing? What is he waiting for?

I jump out of the car and holler: "Oakley! What do you think you are doing?"

He spins towards me with a look of fear on his face. Busted. We have been through this countless times. I can see the lies and excuses zipping across his brow from here, but I also see some sadness that is new. He walks over to me, bracing himself for the dressing-down he is about to receive.

"You weren't at swimming!" I spit.

He squirms and shifts his eyes about, thrusting his hands deeper into his pockets.

"I can't do this anymore, Oakley. Where were you? Why do you do these things? Why can't you be honest? Why can't I trust you?" The full tirade of ineffectual nonsense flows from my mouth. My cheeks are flushed. Oakley just stares at the ground. He has heard it all before. Too many times.

But, even in this moment, I am aware that this is not entirely his fault. I feel like I am playing a part that doesn't fit anymore for either of us. I know he doesn't want to do this, not really. He wants my husband and me to be proud of him, but he can't manage to follow all the rules. Adventure just calls to him like the Sirens of the Odyssey. He needs more stimulation, more variety, more intensity than most. It isn't even that he doesn't like swimming; it's just that he is always looking for more. The routine of everyday mainstream has never been enough for him, and right now, it doesn't feel like it is enough for me either. We are chafing at our bits.

I realize that it is time for a change, a big one. I am acutely aware that our lifelong pattern—him running and me chasing—is getting us nowhere. Neither of us is happy with this pattern, and the stakes are becoming too high. I know that one day I will not be able to catch him. And then what?

I love life. I love my family. I love the blue sky, and I love this planet. So does Oakley. It would be a terrible waste to force ourselves to remain in this unhealthy pattern until we lose this, our joy for life and our love. So in this moment, I decide that we won't.

8:00—I am sitting on the ferry, riding home. Oakley sits beside me, looking momentarily chastised, but I know it won't last. I get a text from my husband. He is in Charleston, South Carolina, on a business trip. He lives well on these trips and has been sending me pictures of lovely scenes—fountains and blooming flowers—all day.

How's Oakley? reads the text.

I am going, I reply.

Twain knows this is shorthand for the bike trip that I have been threatening for years.

Okay, he responds. *I support you, 100 percent.*

And just like that I have committed. Oakley and I will leave the coming summer for a bike trip across the United States. I will close my private counseling practice, and he will take a leave of absence from school. We will spend this winter researching routes, collecting gear, scraping for funds, and preparing to leave the safety and monotony of home behind. We will strike out alone together, and our days will be comprised of biking and camping for three months of nearly constant growth and adventure. If this doesn't help us figure some things out, nothing will. I stare out the ferry window into the night and watch the rain stream down the window. I feel my anger and resentment about Oakley's behavior begin to transform into palpable excitement. I am almost grateful. We are both about to get what we need.

Oakley's Two Cents

My name is Oakley Bradenday. When my mother first began talking about this bike trip, I was not excited. I thought it was a terrible idea. In fact, I hate biking, and every time I have gone biking with my mom, I have tried to make it a living hell for her and anyone else that was with us. But she has been talking about it so much that I am getting used to the idea. I know there will be times on the trip that I hate it, and I might hate her too. I am willing to go, but don't forget, I still hate biking.

He Zips It Up. He Zips It Down.

December 2, 2004

Charleston, South Carolina

"What makes you think there is a problem?" asked the pediatric developmental specialist.

"He just doesn't stop," I said. "Ever." Oakley was eighteen months old. He was as cute as they come, with white-blond hair hanging in ringlets down to his shoulders and blue-green, mermaid-like eyes. As I spoke with the doctor, Oakley was sitting on my lap, straddling my legs and facing me, playing with the zipper on my fleece jacket. He zipped it up. He zipped it down. Again. And again. And again—fifty times, one hundred times.

"I see," said the doctor. Oakley laughed and continued. Up and down. Up and down. "We should run some tests."

Oakley was an exuberant puzzle of a child then, and he still is. He is my fourth child, and I thought that I had a handle on the parenting thing until he came along. He seemed plucked from outer space and put into my arms with a wink from fate, as if Oakley was the punch line in a wonderful joke. That was the look that he had on his face from the day he came to us, as if saying, "Watch me. I will make you laugh and cry at the same time. It is a special trick." And then he would grin devilishly.

He was terribly naughty. He had pica, a disorder in which you are driven to eat non-food items, and he would eat everything he found: toothpaste, shaving cream, dog food, sand, flowers, and mud. He would lock himself in the bathroom and feast on whatever he could find. After what seemed like the thirtieth time calling Poison Control,

8

I added them to my speed dial. I asked if they kept a record of the calls; the answer is—yes.

In a way, it was probably fortunate that he had pica because of another issue. Due to severe asthma caused by an allergic reaction to formula, Oakley was prescribed an alternative beverage consisting of goat milk, fish oil, and several supplements that are normally given in gel capsules, but which we would painstakingly slice open and pour into his potion. You have never tasted anything so vile. He loved it.

He was given the nickname Huffle-Puff early on because you could hear his steam-engine-like breathing from fifty feet away. Twice one of his lungs collapsed. We set up his nebulizer next to a tiny rocking chair, and he would inhale his vaporized asthma medication through an oxygen mask while rocking maniacally back and forth like Dennis Hopper in *Blue Velvet*. He would be grinning and drooling as he huffed away, completely unfazed, but others who heard him were always aghast.

In an effort to reign in his hyperactivity and impulsivity, we turned to intensive occupational therapy. He was prescribed several sensory diets from various professionals. Treatments included being wrapped in a sheet and swung in what looked like a cocoon hammock; wearing a weighted vest; sleeping with a weighted blanket; listening with huge globular headphones to deep-bass, rhythmic beats as he went about his day; wearing a sombrero and sunglasses to reduce stimulation; getting deep-muscle compression massages; drinking oatmeal-like substances through a straw to stimulate certain pressure points in his jaw; massaging with and without brushing; jumping on trampolines; and being hugged—a lot. While he liked the physical attention, nothing seemed to change his behavior.

He ran away constantly. Not little, cute running away, but serious, "Where the heck is he?" running away. We kept our doors locked from the inside and spring-loaded. And when I say the doors were spring-loaded, I mean that the doors had springs on them that snapped them shut when you opened them in case you forgot to close them securely. At night we locked his bedroom door from the outside, but still the clever rascal would see every opportunity and take it. He wore a medical ID bracelet with his name, phone number, and address (think Paddington Bear's tag) in case he was found by someone else. He wore a bright blue harness equipped with a beeper that we could activate with a remote if he wandered off. But still, despite our best efforts, and because a mother has to go to the bathroom or pay attention to another child, he would get away.

On his walkabouts, as we came to call them, he would get into many dangerous situations. I found him methodically visiting every garage in the neighborhood and pouring cans of gasoline all over the lawnmowers and the floors. I never told anybody because I was so embarrassed. I simply grabbed him and ran home. I still feel guilty about this. While chaperoning my other son's field trip, I caught him chest deep in a pond in South Carolina that was inhabited by alligators. After that, I was asked to no longer sign up for this responsibility. I found him sitting in strangers' cars with the doors locked, grinning wildly and pretending to drive. I found him locked inside a Porta-Potty, unrolling all the toilet paper to make a big white nest, his belly laughter echoing off the inner walls. I begged and pleaded with him to come out while a line of people wanting to use it formed outside, none of them very impressed by our parenting. He ran away from his nursery school and into a swarm of bees. I found him on our roof, having climbed up and out of our fenced-in yard. It never ended.

He also lied—told stretchers. He told his nursery schoolteacher that he had found a dead body in his room ("blood all over"), but that his mother had cleaned up the mess. He blamed every naughty thing on his imaginary friend, Somebody. Somebody covered the inside of the car in permanent marker. Somebody set his brother's pet mice free. Somebody emptied all the spices onto the floor. He told his friends it was his birthday when it wasn't and reaped the benefits with delight.

Not only was Oakley a danger to himself, he also had rage. That was not fun. He would not let us change his diaper unless we pinned him to the floor with our knees. He wouldn't let us get him dressed, and when we did, he would just tear off his clothes, so he spent much of his time naked. He would tantrum in public on a level comparable to the Tasmanian Devil.

There were many days that Twain and I were overwhelmed and would declare that our lifestyle was not sustainable. But we were in love with him, so we kept chasing him when he ran away. To this day, he still loves adventure. We kept those headphones with the rhythmic beats on him, and today he loves drumming. We bought him a full-size trampoline at three years old despite potential risks, and today he still jumps and twists and flips and has an incredible kinesthetic ability. I think the hugging helped, but that is not as measurable.

I am not saying we were award-winning parents. I became a yeller, and you could watch Twain literally recede into his own world when it all became too much. As we prepare for our bike trip, we still can't leave Oakley, who is now sixteen, home alone because he is still overly impulsive and has a tendency towards the naughty. He still tells stretchers. Life with him is like playing a never-ending game of Two Truths and a Lie. He still has the need for constant stimulation and loves risky activities. He still has rage, but only toward his parents when we try to set limits. Some things haven't changed.

His story isn't over, and we are constantly having to troubleshoot how to navigate life with a guy like him so that all his traits can be strengths, not liabilities. That is part of the impulse behind this bike ride. That, and, conveniently, it is something that I have always wanted to do. Lucky me. Lucky him? Lucky us.

Should We Do This Crazy Thing?

May 10, 2019

Peaks Island, Maine

My sheets twist around me like a straitjacket of worry as I struggle to get comfortable in my bed. It is 3:20 a.m. I have gotten up to get some water, I have gotten up to go pee, and I have gotten up to heat up some warm milk with cinnamon and a shot of whiskey. That always does the trick, but not tonight. Now that I have thrown my hat over the proverbial wall and shouted out to all my friends and relations and even strangers on social media about this freaking bike trip, I am beside myself. It is as if I am staring at a list of all my anxieties printed on my bedroom ceiling that must be read over and over while everyone else in the house sleeps:

1. Oakley is going to get hit by a truck. Really. I fear that long, exhausting, boring afternoon peddling behind Oakley and seeing him wander across the white line into traffic over and over. My heart in my throat, tension throughout my body, I yell at him repeatedly, "Move over!" until I just can't say it again, and a distracted truck driver comes up behind us.

2. I must leave Twain for three months. I have never been apart from him for more than ten days over the last twenty-five years, and I am pretty used to him. I am lucky—I really love him. I worry about either of us changing while we're apart and having a hard time fitting together again.

3. I must leave my other children. They are all young adults ranging from nineteen to twenty-three. They are ready to leave me, but me leave them? It feels unmotherly.

4. I must leave Cricket, my dog. She is really important to me. She comes to work with me every day. Will she remember me? Twain and I can FaceTime, but . . . Cricket?

5. I will spend all of our money, and then some. This is going to cost a ton. I am doing my best to get funding, but life is expensive. I won't be working. We have three kids in college, and my husband and I still owe for our own student debt. We have a house, a car, loans . . . yadda, yadda. My husband is really supportive and believes that it will work out, but I have my doubts. Oakley and I will be building our bikes from recycled parts; we will beg and borrow as much gear as we can. I hope to get sponsorships and maybe even write a book. We will camp and cook our own food. But I believe the trip will cost us close to eight thousand, and I will lose about ten thousand by not working for three months. It is pure fantasy that we can afford this.

Over and over, I review this list, but here's the thing: How can we not go? Life is happening *now*. This world is not terribly full of hope these days, and I want to commit to an engaging life and all its wonders. I want to invest in Oakley. I want to trust in the goodness of people and not succumb to that idea that I should play it safe until my clock runs out.

Where's Oakley?

June 6, 2006

Charleston, South Carolina

It was a typical Saturday morning. Oakley was three, Raven was six, Jonah was eight, and Finn was ten. The whole family was hanging around the house doing a whole lot of nothing. It was very peaceful. Too peaceful. I wandered through the house. "Oakley?" I called. No response. I went into the backyard where Twain was working. "Have you seen Oakley?" I asked.

"Nope." He sighed heavily and immediately stopped what he was doing to join me in a preliminary search of the house. We looked under beds, in the bathroom, in closets, and in the yard. No Oakley.

"Oakley Alert!" I called. The kids groaned but didn't hesitate. Everyone began looking.

The thing with Oakley was that he hid. Calling his name didn't do it. You had to find him. Oakley disappearing had happened so frequently that we had taken drastic measures. Our doors all had hook-and-eye locks about six feet high, out of his reach, that we were committed to locking whenever we were home. Our backyard was enclosed by a three-foot chain-link fence with a spring-loaded gate. When this didn't prove enough to hold him in, we added a two-foot extension of bird netting that seemed unclimbable above the fence. In the past he had managed to scale the outdoor shower that was attached to the house, cross over the roof, and jump into the front yard to attain freedom. He bolted across the road into our neighbors' backyards and into their cars and sheds, looking for treasures like mowers and other exciting tools.

The house was empty; the search needed to expand. Raven stayed at home stationed by the telephone in case Oakley reappeared. Finn struck out on his bike to tour the neighborhood. Jonah grabbed one Razor scooter, and I grabbed the other. Twain set out on foot. The neighborhood filled with the sound of our calling: "Oakley! Oakley!" Some neighbors heard us and ventured out.

"You lost him again?" asked one gentleman with a kind smile. He shook his head and began searching his yard.

Another neighbor called out, "He is not in here!"

Our search continued. We fanned out over several blocks; no Oakley. Twenty-five minutes passed, and I began to move past numbness into slight worry.

I passed Twain on my scooter. "Maybe we should call the police?"

"Yeah, maybe, but let's give it a few more minutes."

Calling the police is scary. I have contacted them in the past to try to give them a heads up about our little runaway. I told them all the precautions we have taken and asked them to just be aware that if they ever come upon a towheaded three-year-old wandering alone in a place where you wouldn't normally find one, to give us a call. The response was harsh. Yes, they would keep an eye out, and if they found him, they would call Child Protective Services.

Just then, Twain's cell phone rang. It was six-year-old Raven. "He is at Krispy Kreme," she proudly reported. "They just called."

Wow. Krispy Kreme was three blocks away on the busy Savannah Highway, a four-lane commercial strip that is the main artery leading to and from Charleston, South Carolina. He must have cut through backyards and hedges the whole way, or we would have seen him. I took off on my scooter.

When I arrived, Oakley was sitting in a chair happily eating a donut and drinking from a carton of milk. He was wearing his medical ID bracelet and harness, which only had a 150-foot range, so it didn't help much that day. The manager of Krispy Kreme was beaming gallantly.

He felt like a hero. He was. I thanked him sincerely for his rescue, although I couldn't help wishing he hadn't fed Oakley. I was sure that Oakley would continue to frequent this place. I positioned Oakley on the front of my scooter and rode home. He was terribly pleased with himself.

The family had all regathered at home and were waiting to hear about Oakley's adventure. I told them about his tasty little snack, and they couldn't help but praise him.

"Oakley got a donut!" the kids all shouted with glee. They patted him on the back, asked if it was yummy, and wished they could pull off such a stunt. We all lived a bit vicariously through him. Then it was over. We all returned wordlessly to whatever it was that we were working on. This wasn't rehearsed. We all knew the drill. I added Krispy Kreme to the list of places to check when Oakley goes missing.

The Whole Dang Country

April 22, 2019

Peaks Island, Maine

Tonight, after spending the day running around town doing errands, my husband insists that it is time to spend some time with my maps. I think this is because he is excited to begin planning where he might come to join us for a few days. I have announced that being apart for three months is too much for me, so he will try to meet us somewhere along the route for a few days, so I can grab some kisses . . . and maybe cry a little.

I sit down on the floor with my 144 maps that cover the minute details of our route, a big map that covers the expanse of the United States, and a blue Sharpie. I begin to slowly trace the route, city by city, park by park, big wild expanse by big wild expanse across the country.

One of the many issues we will have to contend with out there is my vision. It sucks. Ten years ago, I was diagnosed with a melanoma on my retina. The treatment for it consisted of eye surgery as well as proton-beam radiation. It was not super fun, but I was lucky. I got to walk away alive and kicking, with only the loss of my vision in that eye. Most of the time this doesn't affect me. Nobody would ever know unless they saw me pour a glass of wine and miss the glass (when I am stone-cold sober) or misjudge whether a bird is coming or going or try to read a map. My good eye quickly becomes fatigued, and little words and roads and numbers seem to wander about the page doing pretty much whatever they feel like. It is exhausting. Oakley will have to become the expert.

You notice how big this country is when you attempt to transpose 144 maps across its width with one squinty eye. Drawing it takes forever. Many times, I have to remove my glasses and rub my eyes and lean my head against the wall. However, after sitting here diligently squinting and marking, now I can see it in my mind's eye. It is pretty amazing.

Over the first several days, we will follow the West Coast, giving us a chance to take in the vastness of the Pacific and the humongous spruce and redwood trees that cover the hills. I hear that there are a lot of them—both hills and trees.

We will then turn east near Eugene and head up into the Cascades. We will ascend through lush forests, cross under snowcapped peaks, and travel on to the high desert of Oregon. This section of the route follows a portion of the original Oregon Trail. We will lug our gear and foodstuffs in our panniers rather than in a covered wagon, but I hope we will feel connected and inspired by the adventurers who have come before us.

Next, we will enter Idaho and cycle along the Salmon River, which is rich in Native American history, and begin a seventy-five-mile ascent to Missoula, Montana. The headquarters of the Association for Cyclists is located there, and they promise us free ice cream. I think we will need it. I hope the cones aren't kiddie sized. We will head into the Rocky Mountains and make our way to Wyoming. We might hike for a bit in Yellowstone or play with some grizzlies or bison or perhaps some elk.

At that point, with our legs of newly brandished steel, we will head south again through the Tetons and along the Wind River Range into Colorado. It is here that we will cross Hoosier Pass, with an elevation of 11,152 feet. That high, the summer snow smells like watermelons. No problem.

Oakley is then planning to practice backflips and various other parkour moves in the foothills of the Rockies. Then hopefully somewhere in Kansas, we will meet up with Twain for a week. He is excited to experience the tall grassy plains in late September.

After we kiss him goodbye, and I cry a little, we will head to Missouri and into the Ozark Mountains. From there we will take a ferry across the Ohio River and into Kentucky.

Next, we will give Illinois a gentle nudge and then climb up into Virginia and on to the Appalachian Mountains. We will follow the Blue Ridge Parkway for a bit and then descend down through the farmlands of Virginia to the Atlantic Coast, where we will finish in Yorktown.

The total trip will be about 4,300 miles. We are aiming to get home soon after Daylight Savings Time begins in early November. After all of this extreme togetherness, I'm rather jittery at the thought of Oakley and I stuck in our tent in the dark from sunset (at 4:30 in the afternoon) until sunrise fourteen hours later.

We will camp the whole way unless we find free accommodations. We will cook our meals on a camping stove. We will carry our water and belongings on our bikes. We will homeschool along the way. This might be the best education ever—for both of us.

We will be riding on endless little twisty and crooked roads through the most obscure places. We will pass through Crow Heart, Sweetwater Station, Amy, Colorado, and Sugar Grove. There are, of course, huge mountain ranges, but also immense deserts and grasslands. We will pass through the Wind River Reservation, the Grand Tetons, Yellowstone, and the Shenandoah National Park forest. We will climb over Hoosier Pass and descend down onto the long (and thankfully flat) plains of Kansas. We will pedal by the Mammoth Caves and Hot Sulfur Springs and hopefully finish by the Jamestown Settlement in Virginia.

A friend who did this trip told me once that he would often find himself biking through deserted prairie lands ringed by barbed wire until it got dark, and then he would just jump a fence and wheel his bike over and around a small hillock to set up his camp out of sight of the road. I wonder about the coyotes. I am no wimp, but I'm haunted by that chortling, yelping, screaming sound that they make as they stream across the prairie like a hungry mob, decimating everything in their path, pulling little cute bunnies apart limb from limb and playing catch with their heads.

Yes, studying all this expanse of wild land between where we will start and where we will end is a bit disconcerting. I am truly excited to think of all we will see and experience, but I won't deny that I am a bit apprehensive about the fact that I am really signing up for sleeping under the stars with nobody but Oakley and some coyotes . . . and snakes, and vultures, and bears, for eighty nights or so. We will be okay, right? I have one good eye, and Oakley has two.

I am not so good at details. I hope this all plays out as I intend.

Bear!

August 2, 1986

Appalachian Trail, Pennsylvania

"Alison, run!"

My friend Alison was hiking along the Appalachian Trail about fifty feet ahead of me.

I saw her try to pick up her pace, stumbling over roots and rocks as she continued to ascend the ridge, but her speed didn't accelerate much. We had been hiking alone for ten days and were carrying fifty-pound backpacks, so her running was more like a hurried hobble.

"Go!" I called. She couldn't look over her shoulder because our backpacks were poorly packed, with external frames that extended high over our heads and sleeping pads and pots and pans strapped to the outside. Alison had no idea why I was suddenly commanding her to hurry, but due to the timbre of my voice, she didn't stop to question me.

Behind me, I heard the thudding of heavy feet galloping up the trail. Something big was coming fast. I heard the leaves and brush rustle and scrape, but I didn't dare to turn around. The faster I ran, the faster it pursued me. I was in a blind panic. "Alison!"

We were both sixteen years old. This trip was my idea. The previous summer I had attended Camp Farm and Wilderness and felt that I was well versed in outdoor living. I had convinced Alison that we should hike on the Appalachian Trail for a month and survive off of wild edibles along the way. I had also just read *My Side of the Mountain*, and I pictured us fishing out of clear streams with hooks carved from saplings and eating pine nuts and acorn pancakes to sustain ourselves.

Surprisingly, our parents thought this would be a good experience. Maybe they were in need of some respite from their teenagers? Maybe they thought that I needed some real-life lessons? Maybe I was more like Oakley than I realize.

Not surprisingly, it was harder than it sounded. By the second day, we were starving and begging other through-hikers for handfuls of trail mix. We hadn't even brought a stove and realized quickly that acorns, while theoretically a food, are so bitter that if you don't cook them for hours, they're basically inedible.

Needless to say, we were ill prepared. No stove, no food, no maps. And we were in bear country. We had recently passed a sign that gave instructions for a bear encounter:

- Do not run.
- Back up slowly.
- Climb tree.
- Use pepper spray.

At night I had been sleeping with a butcher knife under my pillow—just in case. But currently, that knife was buried deep in my backpack. I was helpless against my attacker. In my rush, I tripped. My heavily laden backpack toppled me forward, and I hit the ground hard. My knees crashed down on a rock, and I struggled to quickly unclasp my hip belt and twist free of the weight of my pack. I was picturing the bear shredding me with his long teeth and jagged claws, and I wanted to be ready to kick at him. With a sharp intake of breath, I turned to face my doom.

There was nothing. Instead, I saw that my sleeping bag had become unrolled and was dragging on the ground behind me, bumping along the rocks and roots and sounding very much like a bear in hot pursuit. The relief that flooded me could be sold as a street drug.

"Alison," I called. "It was my sleeping bag."

She dropped her pack immediately and looped back down the trail to me. She was covered with sweat, her cheeks shone red, and her breathing was ragged. She laughed and said, "Let's get some pictures of your bloody knees." I posed, and she took some shots. "We should probably sing to keep the bears away from now on," she said. I agreed. Our joyful voices filled the air, bolstering our spirits and making any and all forest creatures run for the hills.

June 2019

I saw Alison yesterday for the first time in eighteen years. We met in a coffee shop called Book and Bar in Portsmouth, New Hampshire. She was with her eleven-year-old daughter, Penny. Alison had read my online account of this trip and reached out across cyberspace to reconnect. As we spoke her daughter leaned over and whispered in her mom's ear, "Is this the one?"

"What?" I asked.

"Oh," Alison laughed. "She has heard stories." We started swapping tales of that trip to the Appalachian Trail: How we hiked with ferns behind our ears to keep the gnats away and ended up looking like forest nymphs. How we hadn't even brought a stove or a map. How in our starvation we took a break from the trail and hitchhiked to Arby's fast food restaurant located in a strip mall. We set up our tent up in the parking lot and ate dinner and breakfast there. We remembered asking a farmer if we could sleep in his barn during a terrible thunderstorm and huddling under his tractor to avoid his very agitated horse that was also seeking shelter, rearing up and kicking at the hard-packed dirt all around our heads. We spent the night trying to remember whether we had ever heard of a horse trampling someone to death. We remembered how kind everybody was and how helpful.

"You will have a lot of adventures, Penny. Just wait," Alison said.

We paid no attention to detail, we relied on the goodness of strangers, and we learned more than we could ever have from a book or a screen. It was terribly uncomfortable, and at times, we were alternately exhausted, starving, terrified, or all three at once. Though I wouldn't recommend our approach, it was worth it.

On this bike adventure I will bring food—lots of it—maps, and, I hope, the appropriate gear. I still welcome the craziness of not planning every moment, but given my track record of chaos, I will try a little harder to give some thought ahead of time to some of the details.

I hope Oakley will sing with me like Alison did if I get scared of bears.

Bike Therapy

April 9, 2019

Portland, Maine, and Cape Cod, Massachusetts

At work, I feel distracted and antsy and have to try hard to remain present. I am a mental health counselor, and I spend my days with clients who struggle primarily with anxiety and depression. Sometimes I love what I do, and sometimes I find it terribly depleting.

Today, my first client blinks at me through tearful eyes. "Look at this," she says, gesturing out the window. "How could anybody be happy when this is what greets you when you go outside." Rain cascades from a blackened sky, and on the ground below we can see pond-sized puddles, gutters plugged with ice, and mounds of exhaust-covered snow that are stubbornly refusing to melt. In Portland, Maine, where I live, there are often mountains of snow where plows have piled it until well into May. They are ugly things, mixed with sand, salt, and litter.

We discuss the impact of a lack of vitamin D, which most people from Maine suffer from, as well as seasonal affective disorder and helpful *behavioral activation* strategies, but the whole time I sit with her, I feel a fluttering in my chest, like I have a little sparrow in my pocket. I want to say, "I know just what you are feeling, and that is why I am getting out of here. I am getting a bike today, and soon I will be cycling across America with my son. Life is ours for the taking." But it isn't time yet, and this isn't about me, so I keep quiet.

After several more counseling sessions and an hour or two of paperwork, three o'clock finally comes. I grab my coat, lock my door, and hustle out to pick up my son and head to the Portland Gear Hub where our bikes are waiting. The clouds are beginning to loosen their hold on the sky, and a spring warmth is filling the air. I realize that if Oakley and I walk to the shop, we can ride the bikes home. No dirty, salt-encrusted, trash-filled car for us to fight commuter traffic in. We will travel free and easy. I stride jauntily through town, greeting passersby, smiling, and feeling magnanimous in my joy. That is, until I get to where Oakley is waiting.

At once I can tell that this isn't going to go well. His black hoodie is drawn up over his head, his skin is pale, and his eyes are dark. I can tell he is looking for somebody to blame a bad mood on. Lucky me. Here we go again.

"Hey, Oakley, let's get them!" I exclaim a bit too happily when I see him, trying to ignore his foul demeanor.

He scowls when he notices there is no car in sight. "You are kidding me. We are not walking."

"Sure are," I chirp.

"No way. I am not. You can't make me. It is disgusting out here. I am going home. I am not biking."

"Come on, Oakley," I say and start walking. He mutters something under his breath that we are probably both lucky I don't hear.

When Oakley is feeling unhappy, he can sound and act incredibly selfish and entitled. He lashes out and utters statements that he only means in the moment but are soon forgotten. Intense storms build inside him that are comprised of equal parts hormones, exhaustion, too many mundane tasks, unsettled social drama, and frustration. I take solace in the fact that these irrational outbursts happen to all teenagers. They always pass. Not reacting is often the best thing I can do.

As we make our way through the city, jumping puddles and avoiding being sprayed by passing cars, he uses the time to tell me everything that I do wrong, from how I cross the street, to how I don't walk fast enough, to how I don't let him quit various after-school activities, to how annoying I am in general.

Twice, I have to make him stop and take deep breaths to quiet his rage. Twice, I have to make him apologize for crossing the line of disrespect. And once, I become flustered when I realize that as Oakley mouths off at me, one of my clients is walking behind us. Finally, just as we make it to the bike shop, the sun bursts through the clouds. The parking lot in front of the store has been gathering heat from the brightening sky, and the puddles on it begin steaming. I have to take off my jacket before I even make it to the door. As we arrive, one of the bike mechanics throws open the large garage bay doors along the front of the shop and lets the growing warmth of outside fill the store.

And there they are. Waiting. All of Oakley's bad mood vanishes as he sets his eyes on his new bike. "Can I test-drive it?" he asks.

"Absolutely," replies Brian, the mechanic. And Oakley is gone. He pedals around and around the parking lot, testing gears and breaks and stability. I grab hold of mine and study the components:

- V-brakes, easy to fix and capable of fitting fenders under them
- bar end friction shifters, again easy to fix and hard to break
- sealed bottom brackets and a sealed headset to keep things smooth and grit free
- double-walled wheels
- Marathon Plus flat-less tires (which I am sure will save us many a dispirited afternoon)
- sturdy steel frame, extra long to maximize stability for the additional weight we will carry

All the bearings systems have been freshly overhauled, and both hubs are rebuilt. Both bikes have wide drop handlebars. In fact, all the components on our two bikes are identical to each other so we can bring one set of replacement parts, use one repair kit, and learn one system. My bike has a lovely purple chromoly steel Specialized touring frame, long and low with a Surly fork. Oakley's is a KHS Sport with chromoly steel tubing as well. Our guru, a savvy woman named Ainsley who is the Gear Hub manager, has worked hard to keep the price of these beauts down by using recycled parts whenever available, while still making sure the components were durable and touring appropriate. Truly, I know nothing about bikes except what she has taught me. I wouldn't know tin from steel.

Oakley asks if we can go the long way home. This is music to my ears. "Meet me at the ferry!" he calls over his shoulder as he takes off, becoming one with his bike. I pay as quickly as I can, then I thank Brian profusely and take off after Oakley. He flies down the road, and I chase. The storm, both inside Oakley and over Portland, is over.

The sun shines down. Golden light fills the air. Spring has come. My nifty little bicycle and I toddle along, getting to know each other, sloshing through puddles and spraying ourselves with mud and grime. I am dreaming of what to name her. *Bellissima*? Tiger? I don't have a care in the world.

When I arrive at the ferry, Oakley is waiting for me.

"There you are," he says. "I am going to hate this bicycle sometimes, a lot, but I like it now. It is awesome." And he is grinning. It is not lost on me that Oakley is still young enough to be fairly malleable and that our bike adventure is coming none too soon. In a year or two, his moods may not be so easy to turn around, and Mama's law may not carry as much weight.

I hope that this is the turning point and that now he will become excited about our trip, but of course it is not. He is not. As spring turns to summer, Oakley's moods continue to challenge me. They at once propel me toward our journey that I am hoping has life-altering potential and keep me up at night worrying that a bike trip alone with him might put me in over my head.

On a Thursday in May, Oakley and I cut school and work for the day and head off to bike the Cape Cod Rail Trail as part of our training. It is a fifty-mile paved, flat trail connecting Hyannis to Wellfleet, surrounded by beautiful lakes, nationally acclaimed seashores, and miles of pine forest. Oakley has been especially naughty lately, and this outing counts as being grounded. Time with his parents, away from the influences of social media, friends, and bad patterns, often helps him regroup.

As we navigate our bikes through Hyannis, I accidentally stop short at an intersection, and Oakley screeches to a halt with his front tire nearly kissing my rear tire.

"Mom, why did you do that?" he yells, both scared and furious.

"Because I didn't want to get hit by that truck. I am sorry."

"This is so stupid. I don't know why we have to do this. You are the worst biker." Again, his fear has transformed into vitriolic anger.

The tirade continues as we navigate our way through town, weaving in and out of construction mayhem and clouds of grit and sand kicked up in the wind from the road work. This seems to add fuel to Oakley's mood. "This was your idea, this whole bike thing. I never wanted to do it. I won't go!" he yells over the sound of jackhammers and traffic.

I have heard it all before. I try to keep quiet, but his biking is becoming more erratic. I realize that we need to deal with this before we continue. I pull into a parking lot and signal for him to join me and park his bike. We sit on a curb a bit away from the road.

"This is just dumb," he mutters. "I just want to go to high school like my friends. I don't like biking; you do."

I feel defeated, but I sit there and listen. Oakley has often voiced anger over the choices we have made as parents. His fury comes on hot and fast over having to participate in sports, play an instrument, attend forced-family-fun activities, and do homework. I want to validate him, but I am also aware that he would likely opt out of all structured activities if given a choice and partake solely in what we call *idiot glee*—when his physical activities rise to a hysterical pitch. We try to make room for this in his life to an extent, but as my husband, Twain, frequently says, "Oakley needs a firm hand on the tiller."

Once again, I take the time to explain to Oakley why we are taking this trip and what all the benefits are. Getting away from the jackhammering and construction seems to quiet him as much as my words.

It isn't long before his fury subsides and he is able to acknowledge that getting away from schedules, rushing, and lists—and the idea of perhaps biking by bison (rather than orange cones and blaring horns)—does sound intriguing. He can even voice that he is struggling to make good decisions. Eventually, he cools down enough to resume biking.

When we finally arrive at the Cape Cod Rail Trail, Oakley takes off like a rocket, as I knew he would. His legs power up and down, and he quickly outdistances me. A flock of wild turkeys has congregated on the path. The males have their tails fanned out, and the females are coquettishly prancing around them. Again, Oakley must screech to a halt.

"Look at the turkeys," he calls. I zoom up behind him. As I do, a rabbit is flushed out from the bushes and joins the turkeys. It freezes long enough for us to marvel at its huge white fluffy tail and twitchy whiskers.

"He is so cute!" Oakley has obviously forgotten how much he hates biking. "This is awesome! I am going to see how many miles I can go no-handed." He is off again. The dark fury inside him is extinguished as he moves through the outdoors, burning his energy and feeling amazement at what he encounters. He cycles a mile and a half no-handed with panache.

How many times will he shout at me during our cross-America bike adventure "This is the worst idea!"? How many times will he insist he is quitting? Probably as many times as he will say (as he did while we ate our ice cream along the Rail Trail, looking out at the ocean and watching the ships roll by) "This is really fun. My bike is awesome. Do you want to watch me do a backflip from that rock?"

Oakley's Two Cents

Worries and Looking Forward

So there are a few things that I am excited about seeing when we bike across the country. One, I am excited to see the world. The places that we are going to pass through and maybe even stop and explore sound cool. I guess this trip is sounding better. I have been out West before, but it was when I was little. This time she won't be able to catch me!

I am excited about biking across the tall prairie grasses in Kansas. It sounds cool to travel through miles of grass that might be eight feet tall. I am excited about seeing super tall trees with six-foot-wide trunks in Oregon. I am going to try and climb them.

BUT there are still things that I am not excited about. For instance, I hear that the dogs chase you while you bike through farmland on very long and twisty roads. My mom says we can carry pepper spray to keep them away. She says sometimes you have to get off your bike and use it as a shield from the dogs. That is terrifying to me, and I think that I should carry a baseball bat at all times to whack them.

The other thing I am not looking forward to is going over the Rocky Mountains. It will be all uphill, and I am going to hate this. I will probably throw my bike off the side of a mountain.

Anyway, now I think that there is a lot to worry about and a lot to look forward to.

Freedom Is a Need

May 19, 1985

Ardmore, Pennsylvania

I was sitting in tenth-grade English class, filled with what can only be described as an insatiable itch to not be there. Those blue plastic chairs affixed to tiny wooden desks prevented me from moving at all. No leaning back, no scooching back in the seat to lean forward, just forcing me to sit and attend, as if my body should be an afterthought. I looked out the windows and saw a beautiful blue sky with puffy white clouds blowing by, and I just knew that a balmy wind was filling in. The grass in the school playing fields had just turned green. I needed to get out of here.

My notebook was covered with doodles. I just couldn't make myself care about what the teacher was saying. I liked him, but he was boring me to death. It all seemed irrelevant. I raised my hand and asked to visit the bathroom. He looked at me skeptically; I had a bit of a reputation. "Make it fast," he said.

I made it fast—down the hall and out the side door of the school. The air was balmy, just like I imagined. It smelled sweet and enticing, and I simply walked away from the school and all my responsibilities and constrictions. It didn't feel like a choice—more like a need.

I strolled purposefully down the road toward the nearby park, out of sight from the school. There was a pond there with ducks. I liked to go wander in the woods and then sit by the water and write, draw, or just space out. The day before me had just opened up to a delicious feast of the senses and adventure.

I was failing high school. I had cut so many classes that I had gone beyond the limit of allowable absences. My parents weren't aware of how bad things had gotten. I had intercepted several phone calls home and modified several report cards that year. *Fs are very easy to turn into Bs.* If I thought about what was going to happen when it all caught up to me, I'd feel sick, so I chose not to. Instead I climbed trees and goofed off, always smiling and acting like it was all one big romp. People tended to think that I was a stoner, but really, although I had dabbled, I was not. I was just pulled to be free.

I was also a pathological liar. The lies began as a form of protection—a way to keep me out of trouble at school and with my parents—but became a way of life. I created fictional as well as non-fictional adventures to keep me entertained. I told my parents that I was babysitting and instead took the train into the city and walked the streets—all night long. I told people that I fell off my roof to get out of a social commitment. I even told all my friends that I was dating the rock star Prince. It had gotten out of hand. As I sat in the park, I fabricated more of these stories and excuses to get me through the next week. I thought I had it all figured out.

But I didn't. The stress of trying to maintain all these stories was getting to me. As free as I longed to be, keeping up these stories had become its own cage. Sometimes I hated myself and felt angry that I couldn't do what everyone else seemed to be doing. Why couldn't I just "do" school? Why had I made my life so complicated? Other kids seemed to balance it all, but I couldn't seem to. I felt different from everybody else. How come they could follow the rules so easily? My lies and stories had definitely made my life exciting, but there is a thin line between adventure and disaster.

I had a group of close friends who often joined me on my escapades. We had cut school and stolen off to amusement parks, snuck into fenced-in pastures and ridden bareback on police horses. We had run away to the Jersey Shore and to a Pocono ski resort, all while fabricating elaborate tales of nannying jobs. It was somewhat of a miracle that we came to no harm and rarely seemed to get caught. Yet all those crazy friends were maintaining their lives, grades, part-time jobs, and basic responsibilities far better than I. They were doing well in school, and I heard them beginning to talk about colleges and their futures. I, on the other hand, had spent twenty-eight days at in-school suspension due to cutting class. I didn't believe there was a college out there that would be interested in me. I dreamed of becoming a barefoot gypsy. The idea of staying in school a second longer than necessary or maintaining a nine-to-five job was absurd.

In the end, I did get caught. One of my lies was that I was on the swim team and that practice was every afternoon from three to five o'clock. This gave me an extra two hours of freedom before I was expected home for dinner. The truth was that due to my failing grades, I had been kicked off the team several months ago and was spending that time running wild. One day my mother unexpectedly came to watch me in a swim meet. I was not there. She asked the coach about my whereabouts and everything unraveled: cutting school, the failing grades, and my cut-from-the-team status. It all came crashing down.

Oakley and I are the perfect match. It is uncanny. I see him chafing, as I did at his age. I made it through due to luck, forgiving parents, and a feeling of joy and belonging in the outdoors. I eventually took the SATs and a test for my GED, going on to Prescott College, which focused on experiential education for non-traditional students.

As an adult, I found work leading wilderness trips, then ultimately became a Licensed Clinical Social Worker, focusing on helping others find out what will help them lead a fulfilling life. I was incredibly lucky. My challenges could have led me down a rabbit hole of academic failure, trouble with the law, and a variety of negative coping strategies such as copious drug use. I don't want that to happen to Oakley, and I am not going to wait to see if he is as lucky as I was. It is not a gamble that I am willing to take.

Biker Advice

June 10, 2019

Portland, Maine

Recently, biking has become the fulcrum of my life. I am writing and talking about it more than I ever thought possible. I am currently riding three times a week with an assortment of folks. Each ride is about twenty to thirty miles long—nothing crazy, just super fun.

Once a week, I go with Oakley, whether he likes it or not. These rides are going really well. I can feel us becoming a team: our communication is improving, we are working better and better together, and our mutual excitement about our trek across America is on the rise. These rides are fast and hard—he sets the pace and then yells at me that we are going too fast. We keep reminding each other that we won't need to race across the country.

Once a week, I ride with my husband, Twain. These are sweet rides. They are not overly taxing and usually end with a beer somewhere. We meet after work and use them as an excuse to get away from the monotony of the workweek while pretending that it is in the name of exercise.

And once a week, I ride with a motley crew of ragtag bikers from Peaks Island, Maine, and the surrounding area. We meet every Wednesday off of the 6:15 a.m. ferry and hit the roads before traffic builds for the morning commute. We are not trying to break any records. Rather, our mission is to enjoy some camaraderie and get out in the spring freshness. Anyone who wants to join us is welcome.

Being immersed in all this biking has put me in touch with all manner of bike nerds. Don't get me wrong. I LOVE BIKE NERDS! I am not a researcher, and they are my best source of information and how-to. Besides, the truth is I love nerds of all types: bird nerds, math nerds, music nerds, news nerds, bowling nerds . . . Nerds are just passionate people pursuing their interests and engaging fully in them.

The advice these bike nerds have bestowed upon me has been incredibly varied and often contradictory. I have been told to get toe baskets for my pedals and invest in clip-on bike shoes; buy Kevlar tires to avoid flats and have Oakley become well versed in bike maintenance by repairing three flats a week; get pepper spray for wild dogs we encounter along the way and carry a tennis racket for bopping them on the nose; wear chamois-lined bike shorts for protection from saddle sores and wear no bike shorts at all in the hopes of increasing air flow to my nether regions; pack all my outfits in separate plastic bags to help with organization and tidiness and bring just one change of clothes to cut down on weight. I have been told to bring parachute cloth for emergency bivouacs and to forgo a stove to reduce bulk. I have been told to increase my speed by getting ceramic bearings and to cart my dog, Cricket, with me in a Burley bicycle trailer. The list is endless, and I eat it up. I am sure I will follow nearly everyone's advice at one time or another.

I have found that the bike nerds who give me tips come in multiple varieties. First, there are the gearhead bike nerds. These enthusiasts have the latest and greatest available bike gear for which they have paid top dollar. They are often seen on the road covered in head-to-toe spandex with wraparound sunglasses and aerodynamic helmets. Their tires are razor thin, and their bikes weigh next to nothing. They blow by me and leave me huffing and puffing in their wake.

Second, there are the hipster bike nerds. They can be identified by their tall dark socks and earth-toned outfits, perhaps including a clever, ironic tee-shirt. They love bicycles with personality, beautiful bicycles with sleek frames and subtle tones, leather-wrapped handlebars, and retro saddles. Hipster bike nerds frequently purchase their bikes from individual sellers and have lovingly restored them to meet their specifications and eye for the aesthetic.

Third, there are the commuter bike nerds. They are recognizable at a glance due to the fact that they almost always have some sort of elastic around their ankles to keep their trouser cuffs from getting caught up in their chain or covered with grease. They carry either a backpack or a pannier to hold their lunches and other work-related paraphernalia. Often, they are seen wearing windbreakers or Dayglow vests to keep them safe amongst the more inhospitable commuter traffic.

Fourth, there are the collector bike nerds. These people love bikes for the mechanical genius inherent in them as much as they love riding them. They often have eight to ten bikes lovingly stored in their sheds and garages and can pick just the right one for any given situation. They may have a bike with snow tires, the bike they rode when they were twenty, a foldable bike, a mountain bike, a racing bike, a touring bike—the full gamut. They never let a bike go but rather keep them archived along with stories about their histories and significance.

Fifth, there are the Sunday-driver bike nerds. These guys are only seen cycling in fine weather. They are not fast, because what would be the point? They poke along, chat with fellow riders, and stop often to smell the roses. They can be seen cruising along on their heavy, drop-handled cross-barred bicycles made for easy on/off access, complete with a basket carrying a bottle of water and perhaps a good library book. They wear overalls, linen pants, jeans, or even skirts and have no concern over whether they break a sweat.

Sixth, there are the nomads, those folks out there who love their bikes because they are the only wheels they have. These people either don't have a license or don't have a car and have fitted out their bikes to haul themselves, and a great deal of stuff, around. They often are seen with converted child trailers laden with various personal belongings or with shopping bags swinging perilously close to the front spokes of their handlebars. They are out rain or shine, just doing what they have to do.

Lastly, there are the fun-time bike nerds—recognized by their sturdy bikes of either the mountain or BMX variety. They are simply playing: jumping curbs, skidding out, hopping boulders, whooshing far too fast down enormous hills, and generally yeehawing through their rides. They are excitement driven, full of exuberance and spunk. Their bikes are often bashed up and covered with battle scars, each a point of pride with a suitable story attached.

I am sure there are more. All these nerds really share one thing, and that is simply the knowledge that bikes are awesome. They are fun, practical, environmentally friendly, and good for you.

As for me, the truth is that although I do enjoy biking, I like the adventure more. Biking is a means of escape for me, a quick way to see what is around the next corner and the next and the next.

It Takes a Community

August 1, 2013

Peaks Island, Maine

Ten-year-old Oakley was puttering away his time jumping on the trampoline. He was doing front flips, back flips, rodeos, and the like, elevating himself twelve feet in the air in a way that seemed almost controlled. This was nothing new. He jumped around like a flea all day long. He could do back flips even when off the trampoline; he could do handsprings, run downhill on jumping stilts, launch himself off huge jumps while riding skis, and ride a pogo stick forever. He was never still.

When we moved to Peaks Island after eight years away (we lived here before Oakley was born), I went to the police station to give them the heads-up that I didn't always sanction his reckless activities and that they should feel free to stop him if he seemed to be acting in a dangerous or out-of-bounds manner. I was not embarrassed to ask for help and have realized that there is no shame in involving the community to help a child stay safe. He seemed to have no fear, and we have always needed others to help be his conscience for him. He needed everybody to be his Jiminy Cricket.

On this particular morning, Twain and I were gathering a few last-minute things to outfit ourselves for a quick trip to town on the ferry while our fifteen-year-old son Jonah babysat Oakley. We ran through the house grabbing keys, sunglasses, wallets, and phones in the final moments before we had to run for the ferry.

Just then, a neighbor came by with a gift. He wanted to bestow on Oakley his old giraffe unicycle. It measured six feet from the bottom of the wheel to the seat. I had never seen one so tall. (I think this man might have been a full-grown Oakley in his own right.) He presented the bike with a Cheshire-like grin, knowing that the giving of this gift to a kid like Oakley was at once terribly generous and terribly mischievous. I shuddered at the thought of yet another high-stakes activity entering our lives, but I thanked the neighbor just the same. Oakley was beside himself. He cradled the enormous unicycle in his arms like a long-lost lover. Suddenly, I was torn about going into town. Oakley plus six-foot unicycle plus no supervision equaled *disaster*. But we had to go.

"Jonah, don't let him touch it until we get back!" we admonished. "Oakley, we will be home in two hours. Just wait!" He nodded. We ran for the ferry. I was aware that this was willful ignorance.

When we returned home barely two hours later, who should come careening down the hill to the ferry dock, flopping his arms and wiggling his butt in a desperate attempt to maintain balance on this gargantuan unicycle, but Oakley himself. He was covered in sweat with a look of intense concentration on his face. He had no helmet, no wrist guards, no sense. Cars edged down the road beside him trying their best to stay out of his fall line. He was so proud.

As a parent, what was I to do? Should I have yelled at him for not listening and causing me to live in a constant state of high alert, or should I have smiled at him and admitted that I was incredibly proud of his abilities?

This kid struggled academically, he had zero to no executive-functioning skills, he struggled to relate socially at times, but he was kinesthetically gifted. It was the one area in which he felt prowess.

I used to live with my heart in my throat watching him catapult through life, until I became numb. Other parents would shriek when they saw him fly through the air as he practiced a trick. His favorite was to climb onto a railing or fence post then launch himself into a backflip and (usually) land on his feet. I realized that I was helpless. I had to shut off. Becoming numb was a survival tactic for me. I just couldn't be scared all the time.

Forty-Nine and Eleven-Twelfths

April 22, 2019

Peaks Island, Maine

Unlike Oakley, I am *not* a natural athlete. I am 157 pounds of cozy. I like to be active, but I am by no means gifted. I run—slowly. I can't jump. Really, not at all. Gravity and I love each other. I think I can launch myself two inches, maybe three. I can't do a pull-up, never have. I stink at catching baseballs and can't throw a frisbee. I hate yoga. I should love it, I know, but I don't. Sometimes I make myself do it because it is the right thing to do, but it is so uncomfortable. I have no kinetic sense and often bumble through life. I am the one that steps on your toe. My posture sucks. I have no depth perception due to being blind in one eye. You should see me try to put toothpaste on my toothbrush. I believe this is why I sometimes live vicariously through Oakley.

I am almost fifty, and that feels a little frightening. I can easily remember twenty years ago, and I see twenty years into the future just as well. I want to get the most out of every day, but at the same time, sometimes I am so tired that it is hard to find the motivation to do much. I like to be comfortable, eat good food, and sleep in a cozy bed. I want and need adventure, but I have come to love a tidy bed and breakfast.

Forty-nine and eleven-twelfths is sore. It hurts in the ankles and the hips. It's a bit harder to defy gravity and a bit harder to keep up with my children. It takes a bit longer to recover from exercise. No, actually not a bit—a lot. Often, I am nursing an injury from some form of physical exercise: "Oh, my back, oh, my feet, oh, my knees." Not doing too much isn't about being a wimp anymore; it is about being prudent so that I don't become physically incapacitated.

Forty-nine and eleven-twelfths is pudgy. It requires eating less than is fair if I want to stay fit. It means daily advertisements on my computer about the "ketogenic diet" and "unwanted belly fat" and "the Noom diet plan: a whole new approach." Shut up already. Forty-nine and eleven-twelfths makes me have to work physically harder for less payback. It is watching my skin lose its elasticity and noticing that the bags under my eyes don't go away after a good night's rest. Forty-nine and eleven-twelfths feels moody.

I guess I am beginning to comprehend what I have really committed to do. I have been talking so much about our trip that it has made me feel prematurely accomplished, so full of braggadocio and swagger that I can almost imagine that I have already completed our cross-country ride. But I haven't. The truth is I have so much to do before I leave and then so many miles to cover, and I am a bit overwhelmed and frightened.

I will be closing my private practice counseling business when I leave and perhaps embarking on a whole new career when I return. I don't know what it will be, but I know I want to try something different because why not? One life doesn't need to equal one career. This is exciting but adds to my anxiety about this adventure and all the change it brings getting ever closer.

Here is the good news about being almost fifty: I have learned a lot. Even if I might long to opt for Netflix and the couch and a steady, predictable routine, I realize that that is not enough for me. There is this world that I want to experience, and even if this life change and bike trip create what seems like an unnecessary struggle, they are necessary for me to feel fully engaged in life.

Almost fifty has also taught me that for all my moaning, being uncomfortable physically and emotionally is not a thing to be avoided. In fact, discomfort is usually a good indicator that I am not giving up too soon. I suppose it could mean that I am injured or in danger, but more often it is just a sort of growing pain. I do still want to grow.

So I need to get serious. Time to start training and acquiring all the necessary gear. We need sleeping bags and pads, panniers and racks, headlights and stoves, battery packs and raingear, a homeschooling plan for Oakley, and a whole lot more, I am sure.

It is becoming more and more obvious that this trip is really not just for Oakley. It is for both of us so that we can stay energized about life and wake ourselves up from the routine of suburban living and some of the less healthy patterns and habits that we have developed. I need to remember some things, and he needs to learn some things.

So it is time to begin to get in shape. I am going to spend this season trying to get this body back in line. Fifty might be whispering in my ear, but I can't listen yet.

This trip is going to take a lot out of me, but I do have heart, and I do keep going. I have endurance. I have been told that I may not be not light on my feet but that I am a good hauler. So I will haul myself across the country, chasing Oakley and trying not to have my heart in my throat.

Oakley's Two Cents

My Training Plan

Lately, I am exhausted and sore every night when I climb into bed. This is not because I am biking all the time, but it is because I am always very active.

I spend many hours a day practicing new flips, cheap gainers (a backflip while moving sideways), fulls (a spin with a backflip), and double front flips. I try so hard and for so long that when I finally master a new trick, I am pretty much dead the next day.

I have been surfing from nine to three o'clock every day this week, and my arms hurt from paddling to catch waves.

I have been training with a circus school. I unicycle, tumble, juggle, and do Diablo. This weekend we are performing and teaching kids and adults how to do circus tricks at Thompson's Point in Portland.

I run a lot every day and play nightly games of manhunt. Manhunt is like hide and go seek in the dark. We play until we have to come in.

I play the drums every day and have been involved in Steely Dan and Queen ensembles that have played in public. This is exercise, trust me.

Last week I went on a sailing ship called the Harvey Gamage. I lifted 1,500 pounds of sail with a small group of people and hauled a 500-pound anchor from the ocean floor with four people.

So Much to Learn

July 2, 2019

Peaks Island, Maine

"I can't get this freaking pedal back on! Oakley, come here; I need your help!"

"I am busy!" shouts Oakley from the nearby trampoline, where he has just completed his sixty-fifth backflip. "Watch me!"

"No, Oakley. Come now. Please!" Oakley hops down and stomps over. "Here, try to get this pedal back on. I keep trying, and I can't screw it in." I need to attach Power Grip toe clips to my pedals so I can push down and pull up with them for added leverage as I climb hills and mountains, and my bike's original pedals won't accommodate them. I just need to swap them out with another recycled pair. How can it be this hard?

Oakley lightly pushes me out of the way. "Move over." He is annoyed that I have interrupted his jumping, and he is more than a little sick of bicycles, but he's also a little proud that I needed his help with something mechanical. He tries once—no go—he tries again. "It's stripped!" he pronounces and drops the offending pedal on the deck." In seconds, he has bounced back to the trampoline and has executed backflip number sixty-six. I am in this alone.

It can't be stripped; it looks perfectly good. I kneel down on the deck and try again and again. I try with slightly different angles, with increased pressure, with a light touch. Nothing. I can't gain any purchase.

I wobble off my knees that have begun to ache from being mashed against the wooden planks of the deck and fall onto my bum. This is ridiculous. I can't even put a pedal on. How am I ever going to get across the country? I think of all the people who have commented online about how I am getting in over my head. Those people don't even know how mechanically uninclined I am.

I admit it: I am all thumbs and, as I have previously mentioned, not at all detail-oriented. Even trying to tighten the brakes of my bicycle often gives me busted knuckles. I am clumsy and, honestly, don't know my left from my right. I have no depth perception and have a tendency to rush in a most unhelpful way. Not a good recipe for a mechanic. This is going to be tough, but I won't give up, no matter what.

I crawl back up to my knees and try again two more, three more times . . . then I give up.

"Oakley," I call, "I am walking to the bike shop." With my head hung low, I coast down the hill to Brad's Bikes. When I arrive, Brad is in the front yard tuning up one of his rentals.

"What's up?" he says with a wry grin, noticing my obvious discomfort as I stand there, bike in one hand, pedal in the other.

"Brad, I am so embarrassed. This is humiliating. I can't even put on a pedal." Brad knows all about this upcoming bike trip, and he has been nothing but supportive. I hand him the pedal. He takes it and shakes his head.

"This isn't humiliating. *This is learning.*" He then explains that one bike pedal is threaded clockwise, and the other is threaded counterclockwise. This is so the pedal won't unwind itself. So I had been trying to screw one of them in backward the whole time. He laughs, but kindly as always. In no time at all, we attach the pedal, and I ride back home. Problem solved.

I do worry about my shortcomings on this trip. I do acknowledge that I am a bit half-cocked. I am sure Oakley will send me straight to crazy town, but I will carry Brad's words with me.

This isn't humiliating; it's learning. Fenders come next.

The Spark

June 7, 2019

Peaks Island, Maine

I am self-conscious about this trip, and a bit embarrassed. It is such a luxury and privilege to be able to just take off and step out of the rat race like this. It is not lost on me that I am a middle-income white woman who has grown up with a lot of support and opportunity. I feel guilty doing something as self-serving as this bike adventure. Where do I get off thinking that I can get away with something so fun?

Perhaps these thoughts come from the midwesterner in me. My family hails from Minnesota, so I fight a chemical in my blood that demands that we should all be a little bit miserable in order to earn our keep in this world. We are also supposed to praise frugality and hard work and keep a low profile so as not to draw attention to ourselves. This trip does not match these sentiments.

To add to these feelings of guilt, Twain and I have fallen into all the financial traps that our society has set for us, and I am choosing to ignore it. We have taken on tremendous school loans which we may never pay off fully, done the credit card dance throughout our adult lives, and maxed out a home equity line. We live paycheck to paycheck and rarely buy new clothing or gear. We have three kids in college and often need to bail them out by helping them with rent and other expenses. We don't have health insurance after deciding to take a gamble this year because it felt like throwing money away and our coverage was terrible anyway. We drive a 2008 minivan whose sliding doors get stuck open routinely. It is a big joke to watch our children and their friends struggle to slam the door closed only to have it spring back open again and again. We grocery shop at Trader Joe's because it is the cheapest thing going. I don't have a retirement account. Money is a constant stress. It causes a lot of conflict.

Yet when we do get money, do we save it? Do we pay down our debt? No. We impulsively spend it on travel. It seems that every time we get a little windfall, we impulsively spend it on adventure. They are low-budget adventures to be sure, but they are still frivolous and seemingly irresponsible given the state of our finances.

However, this impulsivity has allowed us to do amazing things. We have followed the Oregon Trail and ridden in covered wagons. We have walked on glaciers in Iceland. We have explored Mammoth Cave and hiked to the bottom of the Grand Canyon. We have snorkeled in tropical waters and hung out with capuchin monkeys. We have camped on beaches and forests and canoed down remote rivers. These trips define our family and the way in which we engage with the world around us.

So this bike trip? Totally financially irresponsible. Our money would be better spent paying off loans, saving for retirement, or buying health insurance. But how insufferably boring.

We hear about tragedies on a global scale every day, and I also hear about them on a personal scale through my counseling work. I am often overwhelmed by the state of the world and by the sadness that many people I know carry, such as depression and suicidal ideation, the crushing cycle of poverty, drug addiction, and failing families. When I become overwhelmed, everything seems gray. I get tired and worn and lose my spark. At these times I feel I have nothing left to offer. Then I feel badly about myself and become unmotivated. I know it happens to everybody.

If I don't have a spark, and if Oakley loses his spark, what good are we? I want to be a positive force in the world, and I want him to be one too. The only way I know how to keep our sparks bright is to get out of the gray of the city. To get off our screens and into the outdoors. To engage with others and nature. To stop worrying about ferry schedules and shopping lists. To stop rushing and getting lost in the lists of my life. Adventuring in the outdoors is how I remember where I fit and what I am a part of. This is why, no matter how selfish it seems, this trip is a good thing. Yes, it is totally self-serving, but I am hoping it will allow us to have more to give by filling us up.

My role model is Frederick the mouse in Leo Lionni's children's book *Frederick*. Frederick spends his days collecting beautiful images and feelings throughout the summer days to have something to share with the other mice during the dark winter months.

> "And how about the colors, Frederick?" they asked anxiously.
>
> "Close your eyes again," Frederick said. And when he told them of the blue periwinkles, the red poppies in the yellow wheat, and the green leaves of the berry bush, they saw the colors as clearly as if they had been painted in their minds.

I may never pay off my loans. I may never make the big changes that I would like to see in the world, but I think I can rationalize this expedition by believing that if we stay completely alive and awake, we are adding something good to the world. Believing this helps quell the scolding midwesterner in me.

Bubble Wrap and More Bubble Wrap

July 10, 2019

Peaks Island, Maine

What would I do without them?

"Mom, we are out of tape."

"Let me look in the—"

"Mom, pass the bubble wrap."

"Here."

"Where are the scissors?"

"Um . . . I saw them . . . "

"Mom, did you get that tape?"

"I am going to look in the—"

"Mom, what is Oakley doing? He has his seat in, like, six pieces!"

"Oakley, what are you doing? Hands up! Stop disassembling everything!"

"It needs to come apart."

"No, it doesn't."

"Yes, it does!"

"No, it doesn't. Why don't you cut some more bubble wrap?"

"I am out of here."

"Where are you going? Come back and help!"

"Mom, tape?"

"Yes, I am on it."

"These bikes are not going to fit in these boxes."

"They have to."

"They won't."

"Will Scotch tape work?"

"Whatever it takes."

Last night, my sons Finn and Jonah came to my rescue and helped me box up our bikes. I thought it would be fairly simple, but like most things about preparing for this bike trip, it took on a life of its own. We went through three rolls of tape and three rolls of bubble wrap and used three bike boxes for our two bikes. We dismantled all the racks, fenders, pedals, lights, and odometers that I have painstakingly assembled over the last several months. I cringed with every part that was removed, feeling that it was unfathomable that I would ever get them together again.

When we finished, we were all sweaty and a bit anxious. Even the boys seemed genuinely concerned about the bikes and the idea of me trying to tackle bike maintenance on my own in the future. I found myself trying to reassure them that it would all work out, that people would help me, and that I am cleverer than I let on. Inside, I was already exhausted and overwhelmed at the prospect of remembering which bolt went with which nut.

Ready to start fresh today, I get up and energetically load the bike boxes onto my garden cart and push them through the streets to the ferry. I ship them across Casco Bay, manhandle them into the car, drive them across town, drag them down the sidewalk from the parking garage to UPS, and deposit them into the not-overly-caring hands of a bored UPS worker. I had thought this would be a moment of triumph.

The UPS worker is young and seems a bit too vacant to be handling something so precious to me. But, to be fair, I probably look a bit like a madwoman. I drove with the windows down, and my hair is sticking out from my messy ponytail in odd tufts and wisps, a little like a halo; my shirt is clinging to my sweaty back; and I am sure I have a look of desperation on my face. The young woman helping me is a bit more put together than that.

"Hi there. Could you help me? Do you think that I have used enough tape on these boxes?"

"Uh-huh," she replies without looking at them or me.

"Can you read that the boxes say '1 out of 3, 2 out of 3, and 3 out of 3' clearly enough? I need to be sure that they all arrive together."

"Uh-huh."

"Do you think they will get damaged because they are packed too tightly?"

"I don't think so." Her lovely pink-nailed fingers peck away at her keyboard in a most disinterested way. She avoids all eye contact.

"I am riding across the country with my son. These are our bikes. I am really anxious about them. Sorry I am being so high maintenance."

No response. Finally she says, "Okay, that will be $671.47."

"Excuse me?"

"$671.47, because you are shipping them so far."

"That is more than I spent on the bikes themselves. That is more than I paid for our airfare."

"It's because Oregon is so far." Now she meets my eyes and gives me a lazy blink. Maybe she has her own worries filling her head, because she is certainly not taking on mine.

I feel trapped. I had thought the shipping would cost a third of that, but what can I do? I reluctantly hand over my credit card, feeling my stomach flip.

As I watch this woman drag away the boxes—filled with our disassembled bikes, ten pounds of bubble wrap, and various unidentifiable bit and bolts—I pick up my cell phone and call Bikes and Beyond in Astoria, Oregon, the bikes' final destination.

"Hello there . . . When my bike boxes arrive, would you be willing to put them together before I pick them up, no matter what condition you find them in?"

"Absolutely."

"Down to the fenders and odometers and racks and everything?"

"Absolutely. We do this all the time."

He even offers to call me when they arrive. I may not love him as much as I loved my sons when they helped me take the bikes apart, but if he can pull that off, it will be a close second.

I am looking forward to rendezvousing with our bikes again when they are in better shape and all we have to do is pedal.

Making a List and Checking It Twice

July 25, 2019

Peaks Island, Maine

The yard is strewn with socks, toothpaste, a solar charger, flip-flops, pots and pans, and bike shorts. It is reminiscent of what remains in the aftermath of a tornado. Oakley looks at the piles with concern. "Why are we bringing that?" he asks. "I hate those shorts. Can I test the stove? Where is my flip phone?"

It is a humid eighty-two-degree day, and I am feeling a bit wilted. His questions rattle me.

"Oakley, where are your sunglasses that I got you for your birthday?" I ask.

"I lost them. I need new ones."

Of course he did.

"I am not wearing that shirt. Can I sleep in the tent tonight?"

It is at this point that I decide to send my little whirling dervish away while I complete the task at hand. "Go find friends, Oakley. I need to pack."

So here's the list of what we will be hauling across America with us:

Clothing

- 1 baseball hat each
- 1 bike helmet each
- 1 winter hat each
- 1 set rain pants and rain jackets each
- 1 down jacket each
- 1 set of long undie tops and bottoms each
- 3 pairs cotton socks, 1 pair wool socks each
- 1 pair of bike shorts each
- 1 fluorescent tank top each
- 1 fluorescent long-sleeve biking shirt each
- 1 safety vest each
- 1 bathing suit each

- 2 pairs of shorts each
- 2 T-shirts each
- 1 cozy long-sleeve shirt each
- 3 pairs of underwear each
- 1 pair of flip-flops each
- 1 pair of sneakers each

Camping Gear

- twenty-degree sleeping bags
- camping pillows
- travel chairs
- Therm-a-Rest sleeping pads
- Nemo three-person tent
- tent footprint (to protect bottom of tent)
- 2 headlamps

Cooking Equipment and First Aid

- 1 cooking pot
- 1 frying pan
- 2 mugs
- 2 bowls
- 2 sporks
- 1 stirring spoon/ 1 spatula
- 2 two-liter water bladders
- 1 Primus multi-fuel stove
- 1 scrubby
- 1 coffee filter
- 1 fuel bottle
- 2 lighters
- first aid kit
- Band-Aids
- Advil
- Benadryl
- Neosporin
- Tylenol PM
- tweezers
- first aid tape

Electronics

- my iPhone
- solar charger
- foldable keyboard
- wall charger

Toiletries

- sunscreen
- hairbrush
- deodorant
- hair ties
- toothpaste
- toothbrushes

Bike Repair Kit

- 2 bicycle tire tubes
- 2 levers for changing tires
- Allen wrench set
- patch kit
- bicycle pump

And . . .

- 2 knives
- pepper spray
- math workbook
- journal
- reading book for each of us
- pens for drawing
- . . . and 144 maps.

This will all fit in eight saddle bags—four for each of us—and a front-handlebar bag. That leaves room for food, of course—specifically, all of Oakley's snacks.

Who is going to be so strong? We are. I am ready to go.

Every Journey Starts with a Goodbye

July 29, 2019

Portland, Maine

There are several cucumbers that will need to be picked next week. The blueberries are just turning blue. The tomatoes are still green with just a shade of crimson. The carrots are coming along, but not quite ready. There will be peaches on the tree this year, and plums.

Our beehives are brimming with bees, and the honey will need to be harvested in a little more than a month. The irises have come and gone, but not the gladiolas or the sunflowers that ring the garden—they are just budding.

What tastes better than the promise of a cucumber that isn't quite ready to be harvested or the new potatoes left undug? Nothing.

Yesterday, as I drove Oakley home from his job as a junior counselor at Broad Turn Farm Camp, I found myself distracted. My head was full of lists and longings, and I was feeling homesick even though we have not gone anywhere yet. I thought that maybe if I leaned on Oakley a little, he would lean back, and it would make us both stronger.

"Oakley, I am really nervous about this trip. Are you?"

"Yes," he admitted, shifting in his seat.

"Which part?" I asked

"The whole thing."

"Oakley, I am too. I am going to miss Papa and Raven and Jonah and Finn and Cricket."

"What about Scuppers?" (That's our cat.)

"Him too. I am also going to miss my friends."

"Yeah, me too."

"I am going to need you, you know. It'll be just the two of us out there."

Oakley looked out the window, and I thought that my words had fallen on deaf ears. After a long pause, he sighed.

"We will be okay."

It was the first time he tried to reassure me about this harebrained idea of biking across America, and I felt my anxiety decrease by just a fraction.

"You think?"

"Yeah, we will just get homesick sometimes."

The air in the car felt topsy-turvy with anxiety, excitement, and a new feeling of camaraderie. I was reminded again of all the reasons why we are going.

Tears of Bravery

August 1, 2019

Portland International Jetport, Maine

It is time to go. We are packed and have said our goodbyes, and it is time to board our plane. I hold on to my husband, clinging to him like a terrified child on the first day of kindergarten. Are we really doing this? In this moment, I can't really remember why I thought biking 4,329 miles across the United States alone with my sixteen-year-old son was a good idea. In the last twenty-five years I have never been away from Twain for more than ten days, and now the three months we will be away seem like an eternity. Tears squirt out of my eyes.

"Come on, Mom." Oakley beckons to me, hovering by the security gates. I am trying to be brave and resolutely wipe my cheeks again and again only to have them instantly wet again. Ugh, this is so hard. Twain is drowning in my tears and is ready to get home and dry off.

Finally, I straighten up and pull myself away. As I go through the gates, the TSA security officials look at me with a mixture of embarrassment and empathy. I smile weakly in return and shuffle through. Suddenly, a small alarm on the carry-on bag scan goes off. It is ours. As we are herded to the side so the TSA agent can do a more thorough check, I see Twain watching us through the glass, prolonging this moment. My gut twists.

The agent goes through the bag as Oakley stands taut beside me. He doesn't like getting caught doing anything wrong. "What do you have in there, Mom?"

"Nothing. Just books and our tickets."

Just then a huge cucumber is pulled from my bag. The agent stares at it, and a small smile lifts the corners of her mouth. "You are going to have to leave this behind."

At first I am confused, but then I look at Twain, and he is grinning wickedly.

The agent gestures behind the glass. "Do you want to leave this with him?"

"Um, yeah," I mumble. Oakley runs back through security, gives Twain the cucumber, and scampers back. As our bag is repacked, Twain marches back and forth on his side of the glass, holding the cucumber in front of his fly like a giant penis, strutting like a majorette. Now I am grinning too. As the agent looks over her shoulder, she begins to laugh. "You better run," she says, and we do.

It is a six-hour flight. I let Oakley play on all the various technology and social media he wants. We will be forgoing it on the rest of the trip with the exception of a nightly call home and a weekly call to a friend of his choice. The hope here is that he will be better able to focus on what is in front of him rather than what he is missing. Besides, cell phones have created endless friction between us in the past.

Our family, like so many others, deals with an addiction to phones. I have been one of the last holdouts against giving my children cell phones. My three older kids made it to high school before I relented, and that was only because they attended school on the mainland while I would be working on Peaks Island. I saw phones as necessary walkie-talkies.

My family's phone use started innocently enough, and they were indeed mostly used for logistical exchanges, but of course, the rate of phone use took off exponentially. First came access to music. That was great. Then access to games, which was less great. Then access to Instagram and Facebook, and these apps in particular became real time and motivation suckers. Lastly, to the bane of my existence, came Snapchat and TikTok.

In my counseling practice, I often work with teenagers and young adults. I have found that many people's self-confidence and motivation seem to tank at the same rate that their phone usage escalates. Studies have shown that spending time on social media can lead to unhealthy comparison with others as your humdrum day-to-day routine runs into the highlight reels of your friends' latest greatest moments on various media platforms.

There is also the well-documented detrimental effect of excessive screen time on brain development. It actually causes a thinning of the cerebral cortex and is linked to lower test scores in the areas of thinking, reasoning, language, and processing ability. It has also been shown to weaken emotional judgment.

For some, social media can serve to connect, but nevertheless, 95 percent of my clients report that they feel lonely despite having access to so many people on their phones, twenty-four hours a day.

My own relationship to my phone is also fraught. I diddle on it endlessly, often checking for new texts or emails that will change my life and give purpose and meaning to all I do. I know that the answers will never come from there, but I can't seem to help myself. In weaker moments, as you know, I play Candy Crush.

Sometimes I find myself remembering glimpses of my childhood before the social media invasion. I see myself at age seven on the cement patio behind my parents' house, squatting with my knees pressed against my ears and watching ants navigate a crack, carrying huge and unwieldy pieces of crackers over their heads that waved like sails in the air. I watched for what seemed like an hour. I built obstacles and designed races for them and cheered in a whisper for the champions.

I see myself climbing a fence and running through an apple orchard to a half-fallen-down hollow tree that I knew was slick and polished inside from countless bottoms that had slid through the tunnel of the trunk. I remember climbing inside the tree and feeling the smooth silkiness of the wood under my fingers as I scooted my fanny down through the dark pithy trunk.

I also see myself outside playing ghost in the graveyard at dusk—sweaty even though the air was cool, breathing hard but quietly, heart thumping, acutely aware of every sound in the bushes I hid in, smelling the sweet green of the hedges.

I am not saying this doesn't happen now, but I believe that people live less fully in the moment. And I believe that this speeds up life. I am looking to slow it down. I want to be fully present, and I want Oakley to be too.

Because of this, I have not given Oakley an official phone yet. He is sixteen and desperate. His friends have given him broken cell phones, which he tapes together and uses without data to listen to music and take pictures. He tells others that his phone works because he is embarrassed that he may be the last of his friends to have one. Even so, he is on it all the time. It is like the phone calls to him, and he can't resist. He fiddles with it endlessly. He doesn't seem to be able to see or hear what is around him during these times.

February 3, 2019

Recently, Oakley and I were heading out to go snowboarding at the local hill. Our family does this once a week as part of an Island ski club. It is a great program and gives us an excuse to blow out of town and go play in the snow, away from the cobwebs and dust prevalent in our homes and bodies in January. Typically, I take three or four kids in my van, and we eat snacks and chat during the hour-long drive to Shawnee Peak.

Today though, I have just Oakley and his friend Ryan. Ryan is a great kid, and I love talking to him about all sorts of ideas on our car rides. Today he begins chatting, "What do you think is more important, happiness or freedom? I am reading *Brave New World* by Aldous Huxley, and it is one of the themes."

I look over at Oakley, who is riding shotgun. He is diddling on a phone that a friend gave him, which is not hooked up to a number. It only can be used when connected to Wi-Fi unless you have downloaded games or music. Apparently, he is playing some game now.

"What do you think, Oakley?" I ask him.

"What?"

"About Ryan's question?" He shrugs and grunts.

Ryan tries again. "Did you know that teenage pregnancy is decreasing, but it is still a lot more common in the South than the North?"

"Oakley, put your phone down. We are talking."

"No, I am only doing one more thing." His voice is beginning to escalate.

"Put it down, buddy."

"You're so annoying, stop!"

I see exactly where this is heading. Poor Ryan. I wait another minute or two. "Oakley, you're being rude." Ryan shifts uncomfortably in his seat. He doesn't want to hear this. "Oakley. Now."

"Just give me a sec!" he yells. His fingers swipe, and his eyes dart across the screen.

I put my hand out, gesturing that I want the phone. "Now, Oakley." There is no wiggle room in my voice. Oakley's hand darts out, and he aggressively shoves my hand away. This kid is solid muscle, and it actually hurts.

"Leave me alone!" he shouts. Ryan winces.

I take the phone from his hands. He won't be seeing it again. Fortunately, one of the wonderful things about Oakley is that he knows when he has crossed a line and understands the repercussions. He slouches down in his seat and puts his chin to his chest.

Oakley will not have an iPhone on our bike trip. No YouTube, games, Instagram, nothing. This trip is the last chance I have to help him disconnect from the distraction of screens and to reconnect to the world around him.

So what is the answer to Ryan's first question? What is more important, freedom or happiness? Oakley just lost the freedom of a phone in the name of happiness. Our happiness (and Ryan's).

So as we fly our way across the country now, Oakley stares at games, movies, and memes, and I stare out the plane window through teary eyes. The earth below looks so big. The farms seem to stretch from horizon to horizon, and the mountains thrust up in what seem like unnavigable pinnacles. I picture our little legs spinning round and round over all that land.

"Oakley, look at how far we have to go to get home."

He glances from up from my phone. "Wow," he says in a screen-eyed stupor.

And I think, *He has no idea what we are in for.* Then again, neither do I. I am excited. I am terrified. I can't wait to see how this story unfolds.

On Our Way—Ready or Not

August 2, 2019

Oregon

The bus pulls into downtown Astoria, Oregon, a little after noon. Astoria is a beautiful town surrounded by magnificent forests and the Columbia River as it flows into the Pacific. Oakley and I are wide-eyed and eager to start our adventure. We clamber off the bus and proceed to drag our luggage down one street and up the next, excitedly looking for the bike store where we shipped our bikes and had them reassembled.

In a stroke of genius, I have packed many of our belongings in an oversized laundry bag that can be easily disposed of so that we won't have to try to bike with it or ship it home. It is stuffed with tents, clothes, cooking equipment, sleeping bags, pads, books, and toiletries. The only problem is the weight. It is a beast. As we walk through the town, Oakley carries two of our panniers, and I grapple with the unwieldy bag. Sure enough, before we have gotten a block, the bag begins to give way at the seams.

"Come on, Mom. Hurry up!" calls Oakley from twenty feet ahead of me. He is yet unaware that our bag is actively trying to disgorge itself all over the sidewalk. "I think the store is over on that street."

I redo my grip on either side of my oversized bag and try to increase my pace, both because of my enthusiasm to see our bikes and to prevent any more prolonged stress on the sides of the ever-widening hole. Alas, as I hurry, so does the hole. First goes a phone charger, then some socks, a water bottle, and then my bathing suit. "Mom, what are you doing?" chastises Oakley, looking back with embarrassment at the yard sale spreading over the sidewalk behind me. He is a teenager, and on the best of days he feels that most things I do in public are morbidly embarrassing, but this is too much.

"Oakley, help. I don't need your commentary!" I shout.

He rolls his eyes, but he comes back to me, collects the detritus in my wake, and strings it over my shoulders. What a guy.

It is hot and damp. My skirt tangles around my sweaty knees. My arms ache, and my fingers cramp from trying to keep the hole shut, yet I want to be cheery to keep both of our spirits buoyed. "Where the heck is this place?" I ask, forcing a smile.

"Look it up on your phone," says Oakley. Such good advice, but how can I take out my phone without loosening my grip and losing the rest of our belongings?

"I can't."

"Mom, why didn't you look up where the bike store was before?"

"It is somewhere around here. This is a small town."

"You drive me crazy."

"Versa-vice."

We are off to a good start. After a seeming eternity of peering around intersection corners and asking passersby for directions, we finally arrive at the bike shop. As I lumber in the front door, my arms shaking and various items of clothing and camping equipment draped around my neck, I self-consciously announce to the man behind the counter, "We are here to pick up our bikes to bike across the country on the TransAmerica Trail."

"That is fine," he said, nonplussed, "but do you want to put that down first?"

And I do. I drop the bag heavily on the floor and try to straighten my skirt and pull my hair back in a fresh ponytail. Oakley adds his panniers to the pile and lays down on top, exhausted. We obviously need wheels to carry all this.

Minutes later, out they come. My lovely purple Specialized and Oakley's maroon KHS. I feel a fluttering of excitement, and Oakley's face shows the same. We both quickly rise to take our bikes from the mechanic's hands, and for a minute, my heart soars.

But the bikes are put together all wrong. Even our novice eyes can see it. I inwardly gape. "These look great but, um, he has my pedals on his bike."

"Yeah, these are her pedals, and my brake levers aren't lined up on the handlebars." Indeed, one of Oakley's brake handles is a good three inches higher than the other. I test the brakes on my bike, and they don't engage with the wheel at all.

"Um, I also think the brakes need to be adjusted," I croak, ever apologetic.

I look at the mechanic a little more closely, notice a telltale red tinge to his eyes, smell a skunky funk emanating from his clothing, and slowly absorb the meaning behind his sloppy smile.

Oh no, I think, *the blind leading the blind. He is higher than a kite! Is this the cheerful, helpful man that I spoke to on the phone? The "Yes, I can" man?* I do not love him anymore.

"Oh, wow, yeah, I can fix that. It must have happened when we unpacked the boxes and the parts all got mixed up. Sorry about that." The mechanic brings out his tools and begins re-reassembling them. But every time he declares that they are finished, we see another component that needs yet another adjustment. A feeling grows that we just need to get out of there before we realize how deeply we are in over our heads.

As quickly as we can, we transfer our gear from our torn laundry bag into our panniers and then onto our bikes. It is midafternoon, and we still need to provision ourselves with food and make it to our campsite. We have never fully loaded up our bikes before, let alone ridden on them loaded. We stand on the sidewalk outside the shop and bicker over who will carry the tent, who will carry the bigger panniers, and whether we need to wear our safety whistles. None too soon, we are ready to ride.

We wobble through the town's streets to the beginning of the Trans-America Trail, which will lead us out of the city along the banks of

Hood River. Our bikes seem to sway and buck beneath us like untamed horses, making us crash into each other like bumper cars. The trail here is on a boardwalk with trolley rails embedded down the middle. Not the best for the wobbles. If one wheel gets stuck in the rail crossing, kablam. And in our excitement to begin, I have forgotten to change out of my skirt and flip-flops, and the wind keeps rendering me indecent.

We haven't traveled a mile before Oakley's panniers fall off and crash onto the road. He screams at me in a panic as cars race by. He leans his bike on a guardrail, races into the road, grabs the bag, and successfully reattaches it. "I know how it works now!"

We stop in a Walmart on the outskirts of town to get some provisions. We get four days' worth of macaroni and cheese, bean burritos, and ramen. Oakley insists on getting a package of six razors to help control his unwieldly facial hair—which I have never seen, squint as I may—and a bag of Tide Pods.

"Tide Pods, Oakley? We don't need Tide Pods."

"Yes, we do. I am carrying them."

"We really don't. They are heavy and take up too much space."

I see him growing agitated. "Mom, we are getting them. They have the best smell! Smell them!" So I do, just to placate him. And then I realize that we use Tide at home. They smell like home.

"Okay, Oakley, but you carry them."

As we bike away from the Walmart, we have plastic bags of food strapped to the outside of our panniers, tied to our handlebars, and knocking against our spokes. This is ludicrous. We know nothing! But despite being inexperienced, overly optimistic fools, I know already that we will make it. I can see it in Oakley's determined focus as he navigates a narrow causeway clogged with commuter traffic, tightly gripping his unwieldy load and staring down at the white road margin below his wheels to try to keep from being bullied by the gusts that spin off the backs of passing trucks. As we bash our way out of town, narrowly missing pedestrians, curbs, railroad tracks, and each other, I know there is only one way home.

First Friends

August 2-16, 2019

Fort Stevens State Park, Oregon

Okay, so maybe our stove did blow up on our first night, and maybe that was partly due to the fact that the print on the directions was very tiny and complicated and required more attention than I was willing to give. Let's focus instead on the fact that *when* flames began to creep out from different parts of the stove, and then fully engulf the stove, and then leap crazily out of control, and I had no choice but to scream for help . . . help came.

First, two fellow cyclists who were staying in the "Biker/Hiker Only" camping area came running. They were so nice! One of them tried to help by taking his life in his hands and trying to UNSCREW the canister of white gas from the stove to stop the flow. Let's just say he had good intentions. Oakley was very excited as the inferno grew considerably and the flames crept into the gas canister. The other cyclist also helped by shouting at just the right moment, "It's going to blow!" giving us the opportunity to run for cover.

I ran—to the ranger station, and as luck would have it, they had a fire extinguisher. It worked. Our stove was melted beyond repair, but I did not burn down the old-growth spruce forests of northern Oregon. And I made my first friends.

After borrowing a stove from a fellow camper and slurping down some ramen noodles, we decide to hike to the beach. It has been a stressful day to say the least, and the beach seems the perfect place to unwind. We meander down a forest path that ends among the tall dunes buffering the forest from the sea. We take off our shoes and shuffle onto the sand.

I crave quiet, and true to form, Oakley craves release. As I sit in the sand taking in the vast Pacific Ocean, the dancing beach grasses, and the setting sun, assessing the day and mentally planning our day tomorrow, Oakley busies himself flipping off dunes, climbing and jumping off the iron skeletons of shipwrecks, and running in and out of the water. He doesn't have a care in the world. This child lives in the moment.

The land here is mystical. It is not hard to imagine a gnome darting about the bases of trees, ducking in and out of secret tunnels and doorways. Life seems to burst from every pore. The green envelops everything right down to the edge of the sea. Spanish moss drips, and ground moss carpets. It is the land of giant dinosaur-age trees. As I sit with my back to them and my face to the wide-open Pacific, it feels a bit easier to take a breath. The air is soft. We are here. After all the planning and anguish, we are here.

The morning dawns bright, and after a dry, cold breakfast and, due to our tragically broken stove, no coffee, we hurriedly pack up and get ready to head out. In just a day, we have become accustomed to the feeling of the panniers on our bikes. It is actually an easy adjustment. We have pared down our food and realized that it is only prudent to carry a day or two's worth at a time.

We take a moment to try to pick up each of our bikes, assessing their weight and, more importantly, whose is heavier. Oakley's is. At first, he complains about the unfairness of this, but I remind him that he is a sixteen-year-old boy and I am a fifty-year-old woman: my trump card. I am finding that it is sort of like being a princess in the right settings. He begrudgingly accepts this, especially after I remind him of the shame he would feel when fellow bikers and adventures would comment, "Dude, you are letting your mom carry that?"

This is how it breaks down. On my bike I carry my clothing, sleeping bag and pad, our books (for homeschooling along the way), extra water, toiletries, first aid kit, stove (when we get a chance to replace it), fuel, snacks, and maps. All that weighs close to eighty pounds. Oakley carries his clothing, sleeping bag and pad, our food, pots and pans, and the tent. And the razors. And the Tide Pods. His burden weighs close to ninety-five pounds. Apparently, traveling light is not our thing.

We saddle up and begin our first full day. The TransAmerica Trail travels along Route 101 down the Oregon coast for the first 160 miles. The road is spectacular. It dips and weaves under old spruce trees clothed in Spanish moss. It climbs up rocky promontories that overlook the ocean, endless beaches, and huge haystack-shaped rocks that vault up out past the breakers.

Up and down we pedal. Every hill we ascend takes all we have. Every hill we descend fills us with concern. How fast should we go? Does every down mean another up? Up and down, up and down. We have untrained legs and an untested partnership. We wear neon bike shirts that are a nauseating shade of fluorescent lime. We wear safety whistles in case we get separated. Every truck and RV that passes us makes us tremble and call out to each other about how unsafe we feel. We pass through state park after state park. They all have a beautiful ring to them: Sunset Beach, Ecola State Park, Tolovana Park, Arch Cape, Oswald West State Park, Neahkahnie Beach.

At one point, we need to ride on a section of road that consists of an uphill bridge spanning a quarter-mile-wide ravine followed by an uphill quarter-mile tunnel. Neither has a shoulder. That means no stopping for a solid half-mile steep ascent. Terror fuels our tired legs. As we bike, wide RVs squeeze us against the guardrail on the bridge, and we tremble. Cars and trucks entering the tunnel from behind us fill the air with roars like attacking beasts. Up and up we go, hearts beating frantically because of our panic, but we're unable to slow down. We need to outpace the vehicles that we share the road with, or we may get squashed.

We can't speak because not only is it too loud, but we are also gasping for breath trying to get to safety. When we finally emerge from the tunnel's mouth and pull off the road to catch our breath, our tension shows in our clenched jaws and clenched hands. Both of us feel unsure and afraid. Is this too much? Am I making a terrible mistake thinking that we can do this? Oakley needs to vent his fear and frustration about how difficult this is, and I need to hold it together and be his brave, capable mom. This is difficult because for Oakley, fear equals anger.

"This is stupid!" he shouts at me.

"Yes, it is really hard."

"We are going to get killed, Mom! Is this the way it is going to be the whole time?"

"No, Oakley. Please don't yell at me."

"You have no idea what you are doing. We aren't supposed to bike here!"

Just then a beautiful woman on a bike comes sailing out of the tunnel.

"Hi, guys!" she calls to us with a swish of her long blonde ponytail. "You look great! I could see your shirts glowing in the tunnel. Nice work!" And off she goes.

I see no sweat on her, no fear. Oakley and I both feel a bit ashamed for our theatrics and quietly mount our bikes once again. If she can do this—and look so good—so can we. We try to stay in her wake, but she quickly outpaces us. Maybe by the end of this trip we will be as cool as her. For now, I feel very much like a weak, pear-shaped wannabe.

Eight miles later we pull into our campsite in Nehalem Bay State Park near Manzanita, Oregon. There is a special site for bikers and hikers (as there is at all state parks in Oregon). As we lean our bikes against the picnic table, and Oakley collapses onto pine-needled ground, I look at the adjoining site, and there I see the biking goddess herself. She has already showered and is hanging her washed bike clothing on a clothesline. Shyly, I sidle up to her. Maybe she has some tips.

"You sure are fast out there," I goofily comment.

"You guys weren't too shabby yourselves."

"Where are you heading?" I say, hoping to impress her, if not with our speed than with the immensity of our journey.

"Oh, I am heading to an ultra race in Mexico. I am just going to bike there from here first to get in shape."

"Holy cow, what is an ultra race? We did forty-two miles today, and we are wiped," I say in hopes of letting her know that we too are real bikers.

"It is just fun. This one is six hundred miles over three days." She obviously can see that I am chagrined. "You are carrying a serious load. I only carry a tent and sleeping bag. I don't cook or anything—just eat out. It is so I can pull off 120 miles a day. You guys are cooler than me. Trust me."

Bull, I think.

"Hey, I am going to hop back on my bike and dart into town to grab some takeout. Do you want anything?"

I can't believe that she is getting back on her bike. I am practically too tired to walk.

"Isn't that like five miles?" I ask.

"Yeah, something like that. I will be back in a flash."

After a moment, I decline her offer. Adding ten more miles to this day seems unfathomable, and I am too proud to take her up on her offer. Instead, while Oakley gets busy setting up our tent, I head off to the bathroom to see if it is possible to cook ramen in hot tap water. It works in a tepid, mushy sort of way. When I get back, Oakley has made friends with a few other bikers. They sit around swapping stories and telling tales.

Greg is a sixty-two-year-old building contractor from Florida. He is on his last day of the TransAmerica Trail. He has ridden for three months from Yorktown, Virginia, to Oregon, and tomorrow he will finish in Astoria. He is befuddled by the enormous weight of this night, amazed by himself, and afraid of what comes next. His advice for us is to accept that we will want to quit many times until we hit one thousand miles, but then our bikes will become part of us, and we will never want to stop.

Antoine is a young twenty-two-year-old Google marketer. He is biking to San Diego with his surfboard covered in a Mexican blanket and a solar panel strapped to a trailer behind him. He hasn't called his parents for two days and has just received a panicked message that they are driving four hours to come check on him and, if he has his way, take him to dinner.

Pete is biking to San Francisco. He has just gone through a bad breakup and needs to ride it out. He is biking with a huge boom box strapped to his rear rack that blares an angry hard rock medley in an effort to keep him inspired.

After an evening spent chatting and gathering tips, we crash. We are full of hope, fear, and expectation—fledglings on the journey, happy to have found our flock.

We awake with our confidence restored. If these guys can do this—so can we. We are second out of camp (after ultra-biker girl) and proudly continue down the coast. Every time we hit a small town, I try to seek out a new stove, and Oakley begs to go antiquing. I am not sure what this is about: stalling, perhaps? It becomes a thing. "Mom, can I go antiquing? This place looks perfect." Again and again. At one point he exchanges a five-dollar bill that has been burning a hole in his pocket for two silver dollars. What a deal! Eventually, because of these stops, first Pete and then Antoine passes us.

Pete passes us with his music filling the wake behind him. It seems the bass alone will rattle the bolts off his bike. Oakley thinks I am uptight for feeling it was a bit obnoxious. An hour later, we find Antoine on the side of the road outside the Tillamook ice cream factory. He has a broken axel on his surfboard trailer. He stands there on the sidewalk grinning and sketching a picture of it.

"I just don't want to forget a minute of this. It is not every day you break down outside an ice cream factory!"

Way to turn rain into a rainbow.

Later in the day, we turn off the coast to take a little shortcut that will save us from navigating a busy section of Route 101. The shortcut takes us through a narrow forest corridor and on into a vast clear cut. The view is startling. It is as if the majestic forests are a façade for the tourists, and behind them are endless graveyards. Oakley and I are both jarred by this realization. It is eerie to bike through all this death and destruction. Mile after mile, hill after hill, nothing but stumps and scrawny vegetation that look fatigued at even the prospect of gaining purchase on this scarred land. Suddenly, the paved road turns to gravel. Can this be right? Cycling on gravel on a fully loaded touring bike is not easy, and now, without the cool leafy shade of the coastal trees, it is also hot.

"Mom, we are lost."

"No, we are not," I reply with false assurance. Inside I feel a rising panic. This will be the first time of many that I question my map skills, I am sure, and I berate myself for my inattention to detail yet again. I do have the best intentions . . .

Now I try to cover my panic with a cocky self-confidence in an effort to avoid Oakley's wrath. After our teeth rattle in their sockets for another mile or so, and Oakley continues to harangue me with doubt, I pull off the side of the road to recheck the maps. They are so tiny! Each map covers around thirty miles and fits in the palm of my hand. They wouldn't put us on gravel, would they? I'm very unsure, but going back seems too daunting to contemplate. I look up at Oakley and say, "This is right, no worries." Sometimes I believe that optimism alone will pave the way (no pun intended—I promise) to wherever we want to go. Often, I am wrong.

Half an hour later we are still slogging through the clear cut, and I am about ready to admit defeat when out of nowhere runs a little shih tzu, followed by some Pekingese-y thing, a miniature poodle, a dachshund, a min pin, and several other unidentifiable rat dogs—seven in total. What are these toy dogs doing out here in this lunar landscape? Oakley stops short. "Mom!"

Just then a very small, toothless woman comes out from behind some rocks. "Good morning!" she says. "Don't mind my babies." She crosses the road and continues on with the dogs yapping about her ankles.

"What the heck?" questions Oakley.

"Well, she couldn't have come out of nowhere. We must almost be there."

"Or she is a witch trying to lure us someplace awful."

"Impossible, we already are someplace awful."

We continue, full of uncertainty, for a few more miles and then are blissfully spit back out onto the coastal route. Soon we reach our campsite. Waiting there are Pete and Antione. "What did you think of that crazy gravel road?" I ask incredulously.

"What gravel road?' asks Pete.

"I didn't see any gravel road," comments Antoine. Apparently, this time optimism worked.

Pete and Antoine share their dinners with us in return for Oakley's entertainment because they feel sorry that we don't have any means to cook. He heralds them with tales and tricks while I rub my sore knees.

At sunset, we walk to the beach. Oakley runs up and down the dunes and does backflips while I gaze at the enormity of the Pacific. I feel like we have been gone forever, and it has only been three days.

Straight out of the campsite we bike from sea-level elevation to eight hundred feet in an acute two miles. Boy, are we proud: eight hundred feet! That is something for us neophytes. The cool morning caresses our cheeks and eyelids, and as we zoom down the other side, both of us express amazement at how we already feel stronger, already feel more at ease on our bikes. Our excitement for this trip is growing. We are flanked by the sea on our right and old growth on our left. When we pull into the town of Sandlake, Oregon, we are already heady with the beauty of it all and are surprised to find that it gets even better.

Sandlake is nestled between the Pacific on one side and the green hills rising up and away from the Tillamook Coast on the other. The town seems to be ephemeral, built on a shifting foundation of white sand. There are thousands of acres of towering sand dunes, the tallest of which is over five hundred feet. There are rocky promontories, caves, and long sandy beaches—a dreamlike playground to Oakley. The tidepools here are full of sea anemones, urchins, mussels, and starfish—a dreamlike playground for me.

Oakley and I lock our bikes and run off to chase our passions. I go to the tide pools, wade into them, and poke and prod every little creature I find. The fecundity of life is incredible. I let the anemones close around my finger, put a starfish on my cheek to feel its wriggling feet, and collect sand dollars in the freezing water.

Oakley runs off to do his flips on the dunes. As luck would have it, he comes upon a group of six boys all practicing their flipping techniques on the forgiving sand. He joins them readily, and when I finally go find him to tell him that it is time to move on because we have miles to go, they are all flipping in unison, laughing, and slapping each other on the back like the oldest of friends.

Our ride along the Pacific is coming to a close, so we feel compelled to climb to the top of the highest dune and sit looking at the sea and the coast stretching out forever into the mists of the northwest. We both feel sad to be heading east, away from all this, even though that is the way home. For the first time, I am struck that this will be all over way too soon. Rather than run and jump down the dune on our way back to our bikes, we drag our feet, both knowing that we won't be back for a very long time.

We have one more glimpse at the Pacific from a turnout on the highway high above the coast. We stop to take one more wistful look and acknowledge that we are now diverging from our fellow biker pals and will be on our own again. We already miss their comradery and feel the chill of loneliness. Just then a minivan pulls up. Out pops a middle-aged woman with flowered shorts, large sunglasses, and a big smile.

"Where are you two off to?" she asks, ogling our heavily loaded bags and sweaty brows. "You are awfully heavily loaded up."

"We are biking to Virginia," Oakley reports nonchalantly.

"*Virginia*, Virginia?" she asks incredulously.

"Yup."

"Well, my land! Honey, come over here! These two are biking to Virginia! I need to give them something. That is just too incredible!" Her husband joins her and holds out her pocketbook. She opens it and rifles through various brochures, sunscreens, and lip balms. "Here, all I have is a twenty. Use it to feed yourself. You are already too skinny! My lands."

"Thank you," replies Oakley. These moments fill him with a visible pride and add fuel to his weary legs. He beams.

Minutes later we stop to purchase granola bars from a convenience store. There, two men in full spandex and clip-on bike shoes are standing in line at the counter. Gearhead bike nerds, complete with wraparound sunglasses and shaved calves. They too ask us where we are headed, and when we tell them, they begin handing Oakley their bags of chips, some power bars, and their leftover fish chowder.

"A granola bar! Are you kidding!? This boy needs to eat, Mom! He needs four to five thousand calories a day just to maintain, and he is already thin."

Oakley shoots me a triumphant look. It is true that he is always hungry, and I am always saying, "You just ate." These men are speaking his language, and he is never going to let me forget their words. They continue piling food into his arms and laughing. Oakley grins as if he has won the lottery.

"We got this," one of them says. You get the next thousand stops, Mom." They pay the bill and head out the door.

Biking away, I can't help feeling like even though we are physically alone on this journey, we are developing a growing team of well-wishers from across the country who are beginning to serve as padding between us and any hardship we encounter.

That night, we sleep in an ugly RV park on the side of a highway lined with billboards and car detritus. We buy our dinner at the gas station across the street: Kraft macaroni and cheese. The final thrill of the day is that I can cook it; I have purchased a Coleman camping stove that is hardy, true, and indestructible at a local hunting shop in Sandlake. It is made for car camping where weight and size are not issues, and it takes up most of one of my panniers, but I don't mind. Oakley and I are not made for tiny, fussy things. We are big-picture people with powerful legs, and food is becoming our number-one priority. What are a few more pounds to my load? We heap the hot food into our small blue plastic bowls again and again until we are satiated and our bellies swell like suckling pigs.

We are tired. Today we will only ride thirty miles to help our bodies adjust to this new punishing routine. I am trying hard to avoid an injury from too much too soon. I am an old lady—make that *princess*—after all. By early afternoon, we make it to Independence, the hop capital of the world, and cast about for our afternoon's entertainment. Gleefully, we see that both ice cream and the new *Lion King* movie are readily available. But first, we need to find a place to call home and set up our camp.

Our map directs us to a city park that lies on the bank of the Willamette River. It is a nice park, featuring a boating ramp and a playground, tucked away from the hustle and bustle of the town but still close enough to make it an easy stroll. There is no campground here, just a sign that says "Bikers Welcome" next to a grass-and-dirt parking lot. It seems like we will be the only campers tonight. We take a quick jump into the river in our biking clothes to serve simultaneously as a shower and laundry. Too late I see that we are drawing the attention of the locals. By the time I whip up a stir fry and Oakley sets up the tent, we have collected a small posse of curious interlopers.

"You guys are camping here?" asks a ragtag, grungy teen.

"Yup."

"Just you two?"

"Yup."

"Where are you going.? Where do you live? What do you have in your panniers?"

For the first time I feel a bit exposed. Everything we need is scattered around us. There is no way to lock it all up and keep it safe. When the crowd drifts off a bit, I whisper to Oakley, "I am not sure about going to a movie. I am a bit worried about our stuff."

"What? Mom, it is fine! They are nice. Why are you so uptight?" He is so excited to sit in the cool theater and just be entertained that I can't let him down. I can't let myself down. Two hours in a plush chair with air conditioning and my feet up sounds like heaven. I decide that I probably am being uptight, and I also want to have faith in the goodness of people, so as soon as we clean up from dinner, we head to the movie.

It is dark when the movie lets out. The town is empty other than a few stragglers finding their way home. It is time for us to find our way back to our little tent. We walk back and see it, tucked back against some foliage in the corner. Our tent looks so lonely and vulnerable. Just a green, thin piece of fabric stretched taut between some flimsy aluminum poles. There is not a sound except for the hum of the river, sort of like a white-noise machine made for cancelling out the ability to hear other sounds. One could make quite a noise out there in the shrubs of the city park and the sound of the Willamette River would drown it out.

After brushing our teeth and getting ready for bed, we crawl into our tent. I am trying hard not to let Oakley absorb my increasing anxiety. I begin to read aloud from *The Winter People* by Joseph Bruchac. It has been assigned by Oakley's high school English class as required reading while we are away. Maybe it will take my mind off this vulnerable feeling that I am battling. I read aloud about the massacre of an Abenaki village in Maine by the British that took place under the cover of darkness. While the Abenaki slept defenselessly in their homes, the British set the buildings on fire. When the Abenaki tried to run, they were shot down: men, women, and children.

Several times, I hear a noise outside the tent and pause in my reading.

"Mom, what?" Oakley asks. I see my fear beginning to be reflected back at me in his eyes despite my attempts to hide it.

"Oh, nothing. Heard a squirrel or something."

"What are you worried about?"

"Nothing."

"Mom, nothing is going to happen to us. You don't need to be so nervous."

I read on haltingly, one eye on the words and another casting about the shadows of the leaves that the moonlight casts on our tent. We are incredibly vulnerable; there is no denying it. Nobody is around. I could scream out here and the sound of the river would drown it out. After a few more minutes, I can read no more because I feel compelled to turn my attention to listening.

"Wow, am I tired," I say as cheerfully as I can. "Lights out. Good night, Oakley."

After turning off our headlamps, we lay on our backs in our bags. I hold my cellphone on my chest, just in case. It is one thing to feel afraid and turn to your partner for reassurance and support. It is another to feign bravery enough to carry you both though. Oakley begins to snore beside me. I lie for hours with my heart pounding, my hair prickling on my scalp, and my ears sweating from the strain of listening.

I have lived this before. Too many times.

April 1, 2007

Twelve years ago, lightning flashed and thunder boomed in the distance as we pulled into our campsite in inland Florida. It was still sunny overhead, but not for long. The park where we chose to spend the night was beautiful. It featured a freshwater spring that bubbled up from an underground river into a limestone pool. Perfect for cooling off after a long drive. Finn, Jonah, Raven, Oakley, and I all tumbled out of the car, excited to stretch our legs and explore this new, fascinating natural wonder. Once again, I had left my husband home to work and decided to take the kids on a grand adventure, this time a five-week camping trip in Florida to get us away from the dreariness of mud season in Maine. Basically, we were seeking warmth, and there we found it.

Immediately, Finn and Jonah grabbed a large bucket and began trying to collect the little green anole lizards that scurried across the crunchy oak leaves covering the ground. They had been collecting the lizards everywhere we went. Sometimes they raced them, sometimes they had contests to see who could catch more, and sometimes they let the lizards bite their earlobes. The lizard's tiny toothless mouths clamped on tightly, looking like beautiful jade earrings.

Raven was on tent detail with me. She knew the drill, and even at just seven years old, she could expertly set up our tent in no time at all. Together we laid it out on the ground and began hammering in the stakes, all the while keeping an eye on Oakley, who, at four, was entertaining himself by munching on a box of Honey Nut Cheerios.

We had been driving through the South for a month, camping along the way, on a homeschooling expedition. We spent time in the Great Smoky National Forest, at the "Riviera of the South" in Alabama, and in the panhandle of Florida. Before we left home, the kids planned the itinerary and the food and organized chore charts for our adventure, all in the name of homeschooling lessons. Now, a month in, we were working as a tight team.

However, there was one problem. A string of violent thunderstorms had been chasing us across the South. Every day, I called home to get weather forecasts from Twain (this was in the days before iPhones), and he helplessly reported again and again that we were going to get slammed by yet another horrendous weather system. Just about every night, we had to camp in torrents of rain. A few nights ago, we were literally floating on our air mattresses as three inches of puddle formed below. I was trying to keep a good attitude, but I was tired, and with the lightning and thunder in the distance, I knew we were in for it again.

When Raven and I finished setting up the tent, we all grabbed our suits and headed for the spring to try to get a swim in before the approaching storm. The air was thick and humid, and the water in the spring was a constant 72 degrees and tropically clear (like all the springs throughout central Florida). It felt incredible after a day of driving in a cramped car full of wiggly kids. I bobbed about with Oakley while Finn, Jonah, and Raven entertained themselves, diving to the bottom with a snorkel mask, bringing up cool rocks. The spring was full of other swimming campers, and I took solace in the fact that tonight, even if it would be a bit wet, we would have the company of other campers, so the forecast couldn't be too bad.

However, the sky was darkening, and as I looked around, I found that the numbers of would-be campers had dwindled considerably. This made me a little anxious. I called the kids back to the campsite, where we rustled up a quick dinner of spaghetti just as the first fat raindrops began to fall. While we inhaled our spaghetti, we watched one family after another roll up their tents and drive away, and by the time we finished cleaning up, I realized with a sickening feeling that we were all alone—except for one lone monster pickup truck.

The rain forced us into our tent as thunder and lightning filled the air. I tried to ease the building tension the storm brought by reading out loud to everybody, but we were all distracted by the increasingly violent weather. Then we heard a revving engine. At first, I thought that it was just that last remaining pickup truck leaving, but then I realized that it wasn't leaving. In fact, it began to do donuts around the campsite, skidding through the mud and roaring its way through the woods.

It was getting darker and darker, and my headlamp was providing the only light, making our tent glow and perhaps drawing attention that I didn't want in the process.

I announced that we should all go to sleep, and hopefully when we woke up, it would be a beautiful day again filled with swimming and catching lizards. I turned out my headlamp. Everyone tried to settle in their bags, but between the thunder and the sound of the revving truck engine, we were all a bit tense. The truck came closer, seeming to circle us like a shark, and its headlights lit up our tent again and again, making visible the fear on all our faces. Finn was old enough, at twelve, to be truly worried. He knew that his mama couldn't protect him from everything. "What are they doing out there?" he asked nervously.

"Just goofing off," I replied as the truck seemed to circle us for the twentieth time. "Go to sleep." I was trying to be reassuring, but the kids could feel my anxiety like static in the air. Suddenly the truck stopped, right next to the tent. The headlights illuminated everybody for an instant and then turned off.

"Mom?" questioned Jonah.

"Sshhh." I lay completely still. I was willing them to leave us and our tent alone. I heard nothing. It was pitch black in the tent as the thunder boomed overhead. I held my tiny flip phone on my chest and dialed 911, then put my finger on the call button. I thought, *Should I push it?* Still nothing. What were they doing out there? Whose idea was this anyway? I had no defense, and my children lay beside me. Thankfully, Oakley was asleep, but everyone else was taut with fear.

"I am just going to sneak out there and see what they are doing," I whispered to Finn, the closest thing to a co-leader that I had.

"What?" he silently hissed, grabbing my arm. "That is what you don't do! That is what they do in movies, and you are not doing that!"

"Okay, okay. I won't. I promise." We lay there, sweating, hearts thumping, skin prickling, for what seemed like hours. The storm passed. Still the truck didn't move. Finally, we drifted off to sleep with my phone still open on my chest and my finger on the call button.

In the morning I came into a foggy consciousness. My head was aching, rain was pouring down, and the tent and our sleeping bags were soaked through. I unzipped the tent and peered out. The campsite was deserted, and the truck was gone. I sent Raven and Oakley to sit in the car while Jonah, Finn, and I quickly loaded the sleeping bags and tent into the trunk of the car, not even stuffing the soggy messes into their respective storage bags. Nobody spoke. We got into the car and drove off just as fast as we could.

"The people in the truck were probably just having a make-out session!" I joked to Finn. That kind of humor was usually right up his alley. He blinked slowly at me and leaned his head against the car door. He wasn't ready to laugh yet.

At the first town, I tried to win them over with breakfast in a real restaurant while we dried all of our belongings in a laundromat. It sort of worked. Safe, with another story to tell, we traveled on, wondering what adventures Georgia would hold for us.

Now, eleven years later, my kids seem to have forgiven me, and that five-week camping expedition has become one of the many things that created a bond between and an identity for our children.

Just the other day when I asked Jonah, who is now twenty-one, what I should write about, he said, "Write more forced-family-fun adventures. I think those are what make our family interesting." Maybe that isn't forgiveness, but if I am not mistaken, I do hear a little bit of pride.

Now though, on the side of the Willamette River, I feel all the old fear rushing back. Traveling as a single woman highlights how vulnerable I am. I make an oath to myself that for the rest of this trip, we either sleep where there is no one but bears to harass us or amongst human crowds to keep us safe.

When Oakley and I awake in the morning, my head throbs with a fear hangover, and as I look around, I am surprised that I let my imagination run so wild.

"I told you we would be fine." Oakley smirks.

We leave the tall spruces of the coast behind and enter the Willamette Valley. Ahead lie rich fertile plains that extend from the Pacific Ocean to the Cascade Mountains. Now instead of majestic spruce trees, we cycle by towering hay bales, some of which are stacked twenty bales high and six across. They look like skyscrapers sprouting up from the fields. The air is filled with chaff and dust stirred up by monstrous combines that troll back and forth across the fields. Hawks perch along the fields' borders, supping on all the varmints that the machines flush out. The hawks are fat and happy and make a cry that stops Oakley in his tracks.

"That is the most beautiful sound, Mom."

Tonight, we make it to an RV campground in Eugene. Again, it is not pretty. We have been warned of bike thieves and ne'er-do-wells in the area and told to keep everything locked and our gear stowed inside our tent with us. But tonight, with the happy, humming sound of RV generators to the left and right of us, I sleep heavy and hard.

The water of the McKenzie River is a translucent blue. It runs down the flanks of the Cascade Mountains collecting water from snowcapped peaks and glacial runoff. The river's clarity creates a porthole to an underwater paradise. Oakley and I stop again and again along the banks and on bridges to ogle at the fish and plants under the water that sways them gently to and fro. Today there is no rush.

As we stare down into the water, we can see the pink sides of trout as they nap in the calm eddies, the weightless plant fronds in the current, and bubbles tumbling down from small waterfalls. The rocks on the bottom are smoothed by the endless sanding of the river's flow, and every cove is filled with rounded pebbles of pastel hues: blue, pink, emerald, and graphite. For fifty-six miles we slowly climb up and away from the Oregon coast through verdant trees dripping with moss along the river's side.

It is a mecca for white-water enthusiasts and fly fishermen. It is a land of all-terrain vehicles, boat trailers, and brew pubs. There is no shoulder on the road.

As we huff and puff our way up the flank of the Cascade Mountains, the unthinkable happens. My "unpoppable" Kevlar tire . . . pops. How could this happen? I have been living in fear of this happening because they are notoriously difficult to change, and now here we are with a big, fat staple piercing clean through the tire.

I slump. Oakley laughs.

"This is going to be such a pain," I grumble.

"Give it here," he says. I appreciate his willingness to help but doubt his abilities. Usually, even when he starts out with the best intentions, his frustration and lack of focus spiral into an ugly temper tantrum and lengthy bad mood. Oakley would be described as someone with anger issues, but more clinically speaking, he just has a severe lack of executive functioning skills.

Completing assignment without many reminders? No.

Following directions? No.

Keeping things tidy? Nuh-uh.

Fixing a flat by the side of the road with little patches and tiny tools on a stiff, non-pliable tire? Well, that's a definite no! But I suppose I will give him a chance and take a moment to mentally prepare myself because guess what? I am so tired.

I wheel my bike over to the shrubs against the side of the road, dismantle all my panniers, and take out a new tube. Oakley springs into action. Without a moment's hesitation, he flips my bike over and deftly pries off the Kevlar tire. I stand in awe of the muscles in his arms as he wrestles with the bike. The boy is all sinew and tendon, and he enjoys wearing muscle shirts to show off this fact. This is his moment. He is in his glory.

"I thought that was supposed to be impossible."

"Not for me it isn't."

I sit on the curb, head in hands, waiting for his frustration to rear its ugly head and make it necessary for me to take over. But it never happens. I don't help a bit. Within minutes my bike is ready to go again. Our respective strengths are beginning to shine.

At the end of the day, we find ourselves at Belknap Springs, a natural hot spring at the base of McKenzie Pass. This campsite is lush. The Cascade Mountains are covered with huge old-growth trees, and the scattered tents below seem miniscule in comparison. We feel like hobbits in an enchanted forest. Oakley and I end our day soaking in a naturally heated swimming pool supposedly infused with healing minerals found deep beneath the earth. Just what we need.

As we float, we are joined by a group of adult siblings that are there for a little healing as well as a little party. There are six of them, all large in every way. They enter our quiet reverie like a circus parade, shouting and cannonballing and guzzling beer (all of which are much against the posted rules). Their bodies are beautifully fleshy with full, rounded curves, barrel chests, and round bottoms. It is obvious that these people live life to the fullest! Their cannonball contest quickly gains the notice and participation of other guests. It will be mere minutes until this party is shut down. Oakley, always one for a party, joins right in.

One of the sisters has a very long thick red braid curling around her shoulder and down past her waist. She is seemingly demure when compared with the others and gives herself the task of judging the cannonball contest, sitting on the side of the pool and assessing each performance.

"What was that? Put your bum into it!" and "That was a 3 out of 10! You need to commit!" She grows increasingly agitated. "Do you need me to show you how to do it?"

"Yeah, show us!" calls her brother, "Knock yourself out. You think you are all that?" She hesitates for an instant and then is on her feet.

"Okay, you asked for it!" The assembled crowd circles the pool and eagerly anticipates the coming spectacle. Suddenly, she reaches up and grabs the top of her hair. In one pregnant second, she draws it up off her head and throws a glorious wig onto a deck chair. And there is her head, as bald and as round as the rest of her.

"Watch out!" she screams, and she launches herself up off the side of the pool, hurls her mass up into the air, grabs her knees, and plummets, beautiful big round bum first, down into the water. The splash she makes is magnificent, and when she comes bobbing to the surface, there are cheers all around. She definitely wins. Oakley is tremendously impressed.

The sun is up in Belknap Springs, but its light barely penetrates the spruces thickly covered with moss that our tent is nestled amongst.

"Oakley, wake up, buddy. It's showtime."

With no hesitation he sloughs off his sleeping bag and begins to break camp. He is in charge of packing up the tent while I wrestle us up some coffee/hot chocolate and breakfast. Today is a big day, and we both know we have no time to waste.

Today we need to get up and over the 5,320-foot McKenzie Pass before noon because severe thunderstorms are expected in the afternoon. The pass would be no place to be stuck. We are only at 1,000 feet this morning, so that means a 4,000-foot climb over the course of twenty-four miles. On steep hills we average about 4.5 miles an hour. I have been feeling shaky about this, and Oakley has sensed it. The biggest hill we have climbed so far was a mere 1,500 feet, and we were beat then.

Quickly, we load up our panniers with our heavy steel Coleman stove, our cooking gear, groceries for a day or two, clothing, sleeping bags and pads, camping pillows and chairs, first aid kit, repair kit, toiletry kit, rain gear, tent, and, believe it or not, math workbooks, journals, and reading books. We top it off with four liters of water, and that's it. We are packed up, fed, and on the road in forty-five minutes.

By 6:45 a.m., we have begun our ascent. Oakley begins chattering on about all manner of middle school drama. He covers the basics of relationships, idiotic pranks, health class, and hilarious feats that his friends have accomplished. I ride beside him. My breath is rhythmic and deep, and I sound and feel very much like a freight engine. His talk actually helps, and rather than tune him out I ask one-word questions (about all I can manage)—"Who?" "What?" "Why?"—to try to keep us both distracted from the burning in our thighs.

We climb out of the dark forest, and at about mile fourteen, we enter an area that has experienced many forest fires, so it looks alpine in nature. The trees are short and stumpy, eking their way through delicate undergrowth. Many of them have charred sides. Blankets of beautiful purple, pink, and blue flowers cover the ground, every petal coated in droplets of dew. We have risen into the clouds. The result makes the landscape seem ethereal.

Oakley is beginning to run out of chat. I worry he may be losing his good cheer. He has already eaten three monster-size protein bars, so I don't think food will help his energy level. This seems to be the pattern of his approaching exhaustion: chatter, quiet, irritation, then fury.

As the occasional car passes us, I worry about visibility. "Car," I report to Oakley when I hear one approaching from behind.

"What do you think I am? Deaf?" he retorts.

"Just trying to keep us alive, Oakley."

"I am not a baby!"

"Nope, you are tough as nails."

"My knee hurts!"

"So do mine."

"Don't say that! You don't know how it feels!"

Thus we pass our next five miles. And then, just as we are sure to come to blows, we come around a switchback, and rising before us are the Three Sisters. These three mountains are astounding. They have jagged, craggy peaks and wear skirts of glaciers. They tower off to one side of the pass. On the other side is a vast lava field. Who knew?

Oakley stops on the side of the road. He clambers up the sharp, porous lava boulders and surveys the land. He has never seen anything like this, nor have I.

"This is amazing," Oakley declares. We are truly awestruck.

"No more bad mood?" I can't help but ask.

"No way!"

As we hop back on our bikes, the last four miles of the climb to the pass seem effortless. We ooh and ahh and exclaim at everything we see.

Then we are there. A tower constructed of volcanic rock has steps leading to the top. Oakley ditches his bike and runs up the stairs. I hobble after him. And there, with a 360-degree view of the volcanic core of Mount Washington, Mount Hood, the Three Sisters, and the Belknap crater, Oakley does a backflip.

We sit and eat cucumber-and-cheese sandwiches before saddling up and coasting fifteen miles down the other side. We don't pedal for forty minutes. Nor do we speak.

Our first day off is in Sisters, Oregon. We spend it trying to relax but instead end up feeling terribly homesick. It seems that if Oakley and I aren't moving, we plummet into mutual overwhelmedness. No matter how beautiful it is here, it's hard not to get caught up in how far away home is in both distance and time. Oakley expresses this in being ornery, and I express it in weepy calls to my husband. My twenty-one-year-old son at home has done some calculating. He tells me that at the rate we are traveling, we won't be home for twenty weeks—that's five months. That takes us to January. The only answer is to keep biking, so we do.

We pass alpaca farms with hundreds of mewl-eyed babies and fields of marijuana that fill the air with a ripe pungent scent that shocks and delights Oakley. We begin to see mesas that seem to be thrust upward from the land rather than eroded downward. The mesas provide a backdrop for cattle ranches being worked by the first cowboys we've seen. We are entering the American West.

For our lunch break, we choose to wander off the side of the road into the desert. I love the American West and all its intensity: its coarse earth, big skies, horned lizards, scrub oak, snakes, and glossy manzanita. I am eager for Oakley to experience it. We choose a large rock surrounded by pinyon pines and spread out our lunch.

Today we have a feast of granola bars, cheese-and-cucumber sandwiches, chips, and fruit. Oakley sits back to await his food and takes in this new landscape. He takes off his shoes to wiggle his toes in the hot sandy soil. Suddenly we hear gunshots in an arroyo close by. Blam . . . blam . . . blam, blam, blam. Oakley and I stare at each other, filled with unease.

"Oakley, I'm sure we are safe. It's just someone shooting cans."

Blam, blam, blam. The shots sound nearer now, and I think about how far we have wandered in from the road and how far we are from the nearest house or town. Blam, blam-blam, blam.

"Mom."

"Welcome to the Wild West, Oakley." I take a bite out of my sandwich. Blam, blam, blam, blam.

"I am out of here. Come on, Mom!" Oakley grabs his socks and shoes and rock-hops back to the road. "What if that is a crazy person? What if they hit us by accident?" I try to remain nonchalant but find myself hurrying after him. He does have a point. What city slickers we are! Back on our little home of Peaks Island, one doesn't hear such things.

An hour or so further on, we pull into a Dairy Queen, and here we see our first real cowboys close up. They come complete with holsters, guns, ten-gallon hats, and strawberry milkshakes. The shakes match our style well. We sit down in a booth adjoining theirs and match them shake for shake, slurping down these sweet frosty treasures while straining our ears to hear their cowboy patter.

We sail through the rich, fertile Willamette Valley and up over the Ochoco Pass. On the western side of the pass, there are towering pines and green grass nourished by the mountain's rain shadow. We cross over the top, not realizing that we are leaving the green behind. In an instant we watch the landscape change from verdant to barren. It is as if we have biked to Mars. As far as we can see in every direction are rocks and sand. Not a tree, not a blade of grass. The earth looks raw here, and we can see how it has bent and twisted, sublimated and eroded, thrust and sank not so long ago. The perfect geology lesson. Oakley and I stop and stare. Everything has changed so quickly that we are startled. What will we find in this land? Will it take care of us like the fertile Willamette Valley and the coast have?

We careen down into this desertscape, weaving and snaking deeper and deeper into its heart until we find ourselves in Mitchell, Oregon, a town that seems to be here despite the region's inhospitality. Mitchell is located in the cradle of the Painted Hills, and the land surrounding the town is comprised of bands of red ochre, cadmium yellow, chalky white, and jade green. Nothing moves. There are two saloons, three rock-and-gem shops, a grocery store stocked with a plethora of canned goods and a few cobs of wilted corn, and two churches. The population is 125.

We pull up to a little church on the side of the road that beckons with a sign: "Spoke'n Hostel. Bikers Welcome." Outside there is a big cooler of Gatorade, and Oakley delightedly guzzles several cups. It is dead quiet. Literal tumbleweeds tumble by.

"Oakley, should we take a look inside?"

Eager for a piece of shade, Oakley doesn't hesitate. We park our bikes and walk with stiff legs and sore bums up the barren walk. I pull open the heavy front door to the church. "Hello?" we call tentatively. Nobody responds, so we take a step into the vestibule. We are met with a flood of cool air and a respite from the glaring desert sun. It's like a hug.

Instead of pews, the church is filled with sturdy wooden bunk beds, each covered with a homemade quilt and made up with clean white sheets and soft inviting pillows. Instead of an altar in the sanctuary, there are couches and a coffee table with soft reading lamps and several books. The smell of chocolate cookies wafts up from the basement.

"What the heck?" asks Oakley. As we stand there dumbfounded, we hear someone ascending the stairs from below.

"Hello!" calls a warm, inviting voice. "Welcome to the Spoke'n Hostel! Come in and make yourselves at home. I just made cookies in the kitchen downstairs." The man standing before us sports a tidy gray beard and a kind smile. His eyes sparkle. He shakes our hands and asks if we would like to take a look around. If it involves air conditioning and cookies, we are in.

The sleeping and quiet area is upstairs in the nave. There are places to bring in your bike, tools for working on it, and hooks for panniers and bags. Each bunk is curtained to provide privacy for exhausted travelers. Downstairs, there are games, puzzles, and books, a full kitchen with snacks and drinks free for the taking, more couches, and a big-screen TV. There are a shower and a laundry press outside as well as hammocks strung from tree to tree by the river. A true oasis. A bike trekker's dream. It takes no discussion between us to decide that we will stay the night.

While Oakley settles down with a large handful of Oreos to watch a nonstop stream of *The Office* on the television, I sit at the kitchen counter sipping iced tea and speaking with the owner. His name is Patrick. He explains that he was a pastor and that he and his wife had felt called to purchase this church a few years ago with the dream of turning it into a hostel for adventures and wanderers. Soon after, he realized that it was on the TransAmerica Trail as well as smack-dab in the middle of the Painted Hills, which is a biking mecca of sorts.

He and his wife set about refinishing the church, tearing up floors, removing pews, building beds, and creating this refuge. A true work of love. He does not proselytize but shares his ideology through his actions.

"Everyone needs and deserves care and comfort. We are all on journeys for different reasons, all equally valid. My wife and I believe that if we can make a person's life just a little easier and show them a little kindness, our efforts are all worth it." He gestures to the building around us. I also find out that, since moving to this tiny desert town, he has become the town mayor and the school bus driver and has helped organize and run events like half marathons and town meetings for the locals. Occasionally he drives people in need of more than he and the town can offer to cities more than an hour away so that they can find appropriate help.

I have been a social worker for the last twenty years of my adult life. Before I left on this trip, I had been feeling burned out and was considering a career change. Now, after one hour of speaking to this man here in the basement of the hostel, I realize that whatever I choose to do in the future, I will need to continue to work with people to find ways to ease their burdens—one way or another. One hour turns into several as we swap tales and rant about the importance of second chances, forgiveness, and hope.

As the sun begins to set, two other bikers arrive. They, too, are incredulous at the luxury found in this little church at this tiny desert crossroads. As we stand together sharing stories of our trips, Patrick suddenly exclaims, "You all need to see the Painted Hills at sunset! You can't be so close and miss it. Meet me outside in ten minutes, and I will drive you into the heart." The four of us are thus shepherded into his old passenger van complete with faux wooden panels and vinyl seats covered in desert dust. He drives for twenty minutes over steep, bumpy dirt roads that make us comment again and again how glad we are that we aren't biking on them, until we reach a land covered with colorful mounds of stratified layers of siltstone, mudstone, and shale full of iron and manganese, which gives them their pastel bands. The rounded hills look soft, and at sunset they seem to glow from inside. As we watch, the sun begins to erase the colors from the landscape, and I am struck by the fact that this is what Patrick does every night. He shows people beauty and shares his warmth and care. That strikes me as a life well lived.

Before we turn to leave, Oakley does a backflip to the cheers of everyone. Tonight, we sleep on cool white sheets with soft pillows under beautifully patterned quilts. We are safe. We are comfortable. We are nourished.

Prairie City. The air here feels thin, and the sun sharp. The streets are lined with storefronts similar to those seen in old Western movies. They frame a vista of tall prairie grass and wildflowers of red and purple that extends to the horizon. The people here seem separate from the conflict and chaos of the world. A beautiful little gazebo stands in the center of the town park, where a few people have gathered on this beautiful sunny morning. It is idyllic.

Except for one problem. My bike seems to be dragging something. Perpetually. No matter how hard I pedal, the brakes stay on. Time and again I stop and yank on this cable or yar on that clamp, but to no avail. My frustration is clouding my vision, and I feel unable to fully appreciate this beautiful spot. In a bit of a temper tantrum, I pull over at the gazebo and decide to square off with my bike once and for all. Wielding a wrench like a sword and an Allen key like a dagger, I begin hacking away at my bike's components while the locals look on. In sweaty desperation, I decide the fenders have to go. I take off the wheel and pry off the fenders, breaking plastic stays and yanking the frame with little grace.

Oakley watches in puzzlement. "I don't think that is the problem," he mutters.

I think back to his prowess and grace when changing my flat. I am exuding none of that. "Sure it is. The wheels are rubbing on them," I say with false, desperate confidence.

"I don't think so," says Oakley under his breath.

"I don't need fenders. Who cares about a wet butt?" When the fenders are removed, I cram them in their entirety into the nearest trash can, and off we go. It is a little better, for the moment.

Usually when we bicycle down steep roads, we follow a standing rule to not go over thirty miles an hour. To do so on our fully loaded bikes would be too dangerous. I fear loosened axels releasing their wheels, or a sudden violent flat, or a case of the handlebar wobbles, so we ride our brakes and keep the speed under control. Usually.

But today? I am too hot and tired to care, and I have been riding my brakes without meaning to because of my so-called fender issue for miles now. I am sick of going slow. Besides, Oakley has been being a twerp, complaining and complaining. His moods swing wildly from joyful to morose, from enthusiastic to petulant, and from kind to rude. The beauties of yesterday are forgotten today.

He has a habit of biking so close to my rear tire that he actually nudges it from time to time. Most annoying. His knees hurt, he is starving, why can't I carry the tent. Ugh! I feel pent up with his company and with bike frustration as we head toward Baker City. On a long descent, I let my bike open up to shake it all out of my hair. The rush of wind is a balm to my sweaty, frustrated head. I relax the tension in my shoulders and just let myself swoop down the wide shouldered road. I am keeping my eyes peeled for obstructions in the road when suddenly I see a swath of gravel in front of me. I squeeze my brakes and try to slow down, but my brakes are not working well. My heavy bike can't stop fast enough, and I hit that gravel head on. It is deep and loose. Immediately the front tire knifes to the left, and I feel myself pitching over the bars headfirst. I crash down hard on my head, palms, and knees.

"F--k!" I shout. "F--k, f--k, f--k!"

Oakley is by my side in a flash. "Mom, are you okay?"

Blood is streaming down my arm and my knee. I feel like I am going to throw up.

"Yeah . . . " I moan.

"Let's get out of the road. I'll get the med kit." Oakley takes both our bikes and brings them to a safe spot while I sit with my head between my knees. "Come on, Mom."

I limp over to the curb as he opens the med kit. He gives me gauze and a bandana to sop up the blood. He gives me water. He hands me Neosporin and asks to see my hand where most of the blood is coming from. There is gravel embedded deeply under the flesh. Oakley sucks in his teeth. "That is bad. Want me to get the tweezers?"

"No way!" The thought sets my skin crawling.

"Okay, let's go put it in the stream." I follow him to a small rivulet of water close to the road and sit beside it. I wet my head with a bandana and let the water wash over my hand in an effort to dislodge the stones. I feel nauseous but begin to get my bearings.

"Are you okay now?" asks Oakley.

"Yes, I will be."

"You dropped the f-bomb . . . like, a lot."

"I didn't mean it."

"You have a nasty mouth." He grins. "You shouldn't have gone so fast into that gravel."

"I know."

"You always tell me not to go that fast."

"You are a great medic, Oakley."

"I know. Are you sure you are okay?"

"Yes, thank you."

"Good, 'cause I am hungry, and it is past lunch." Part hero, part narcissist.

We eat peanut butter roll-ups sitting by the stream. It doesn't feel safe to bike anymore today, so we camp nearby. There is nobody around, and no cell phone coverage either, so for the first time, I can't call Twain. It is just Oakley and me, together and alone. My hand, elbow, and knee throb, and gravel remains in my palm. Oakley and I read out loud late into the night, watching the sunset and feeling lucky.

In the morning I take stock of the situation and find that my bike is all amok. It feels tender and off kilter, loose in the joints and moving everywhere it should stay stiff. As we ride gingerly towards Baker City, I hear a loud snap, and then another. My back tire begins to wobble severely, and like a lightning bolt, I know what the problem is.

"Oakley! I figured it out! My wheel is untrue! The spokes were loose. It must be from all the weight we have loaded on." By the side of the road, I squat in the dirt and design a makeshift splint for the broken spokes using duct tape, a tent stake, and a pencil. I almost feel like an expert. I look it up on my phone and find that there is a bike shop in twenty miles. Ever so slowly we waddle our way there, Oakley on his colt-like bike ranting about starvation and me on my great sagging cow trying to keep the old girl moving forward.

Oakley's Two Cents

This past week I have seen

- cows in the field
- fossils
- lizards
- horses
- huge mountains covered with snow and glaciers
- llamas
- baby alpacas
- miles and miles of marijuana fields
- too many cars
- deer with antlers
- two elk
- a hefty bald woman who ripped off her wig and cannon-balled into a hot spring
- bear skeleton
- a lava field that went on for many miles on McKenzie Pass
- the aftermath of forest fires—acres and acres of burnt trees
- twenty-two miles of straight-up hill on the side of a mountain that we had to bike
- rainbow trout jumping out of the blue clear water showing all their colors
- cowboys in a Dairy Queen
- ospreys and American bald eagles

Cold Coke and Meat Lover's Pizza

August 16-22, 2019

Idaho

Outside of Baker City, we cross from Oregon to Idaho. The land is big here, covered in sage and chaparral with wide open skies and distant horizons. Today we will cycle to a place called Hells Canyon, cut into the earth by the Snake River and bracketed by the Seven Devils Mountains to the east and the Wallowa Mountains to the west. It is nearly eight thousand feet deep. We are a bit cowed by the magnitude of this canyon and picture the fires of hell scorching us in its ovens, so bright and early we shake ourselves out of the RV park where we are staying. We have learned that it is easiest to love the desert at dawn.

The day starts with a long, gradual twenty-five-mile descent. The air is still cool as the desert slowly wakes up around us; we see a badger duck under a fence and a herd of mustangs mount a distant hill. My hand feels tender and has grown rather infected. There is still a fair amount of gravel embedded in it, so I ride slowly with a loose grip, thankful for the mellow of the morning. There is little traffic, and the road is wide. Oakley begins talking. He is always talking, but today feels different. All this space gives us room for big conversations.

"Mom, what were my birth parents like?"

"Mom, why do I have extra help in school?"

"Mom, will I be a regular adult when I grow up?"

And so goes our morning, quiet and big. The desert is made for such conversations. For seventy-one miles we travel deeper and deeper into the canyons. The coolness gives way to blistering heat, but today it is okay. I look at Oakley in front of me: his strong, broad shoulders and sculpted arms, his big questions. He is in his element. I wish he could always be.

It is rare in our life together that Oakley and I find peace. He is taut with anxieties and compensating for anger much of the time. I get so tired of "managing" him. It isn't his fault—I know this—but that doesn't really make it easier. My tales of his escapades are often funny in hindsight, but as they occur, they fill me with my own anxiety and anger. Never once has he played with Legos or drawn for the fun of it. Never once have I witnessed him imagining with action figures or working on a craft project. He only does big-action things. He doesn't fit in, so we don't fit in. Here we finally do.

November 15, 2007

Twelve years ago—story time at the public library. Ten little three-year-olds sat on their bottoms watching the librarian perform a lively and entertaining puppet show. The children's mothers lounged on the floor by their children, laughing along with them and delighting in the enraptured look on their young faces. Except for one mother: me.

I tried to look relaxed and engaged, but the truth is that my internal pressure gauge was rapidly rising. Oakley was not sitting with me. He had wiggled out of my grasp and was now in the front of the room trying to converse with the puppets in the show. He kept leaning his head into the puppet theater to see where they went when they were not on the stage. He spoke loudly, asking the people in the audience where the puppets were hiding as he pushed against the flimsy puppet stage.

"Oakley, come sit down," I said as gently as possible. I knew too well where this was heading. He shot me a look full of impish daring. I eyed the nearest exit miles across the library.

"Oakley, come here."

I started to crawl up to where he stood in front of the crowd. My cheeks reddened, and I felt unaccountably hot. Why did I ever try to bring him here? Something about the fluorescent lights, the quiet tones, and the cavernous space always made Oakley become unglued. I must have had a lapse in judgment when I thought it would be fun. Oakley looked at me again, grinned, and snatched a puppet right off the librarian's hand.

"No, Oakley!" I half-shouted and half groaned. I reached for him, but it was too late—he was off. All the mothers smiled sympathetically at me, and the librarian popped her head up.

"Uh-oh," she said.

Uh-oh nothing . . . this was just the beginning. I stood up and walked swiftly after Oakley. I did not dare run in the library. "Oakley," I called in my best public I-can-handle-this voice, "this is not funny. Come back."

He darted between two shelves of books and sprinted with the puppet in his hand to the farthest recesses of the library; I followed in hot pursuit. He wove from one aisle to the next and squealed with delight as I gained on him. "Oakley," I hissed when I thought no one could hear. "Stop." He was little but nimble, and without sprinting there was no way I could get him. He seemed to know that I didn't want an embarrassing scene and used this knowledge to his advantage.

He zoomed out to the study corral area and shrieked with unbridled joy. He was obviously enjoying the sound of his own voice bouncing off the high ceilings in this quiet atmosphere. People all around the library were now watching, many annoyed, a few curious about who would win our little game of tag, and one or two genuinely sympathetic. The puppet-show lady was now standing up, staring at our spectacle, and all the children who had been watching her show were now watching our show. As Oakley flew by the check-out area, another librarian called out, "He can't do that in here!"

No shit, Sherlock, I thought, but I just smiled at her and weakly replied that I knew. Oakley spun down a reference aisle, and I started to lose it. I openly ran, realizing that it was the only way.

I closed the gap between us, then lunged. I grabbed the back of his shirt and pulled him to me. His squeals of delight turned to screams of outrage.

"Let me go, let me go!" I could barely hold him as he thrashed.

Tucking his forty-pound body under my arm in a football hold, I tried to walk back to the children's section to return the puppet. It was no easy task. Sweat covered my body as he put up an intense fight to match his intense fury. I returned the puppet and begged forgiveness. The mothers were no longer smiling; many were averting their eyes. I realized that I could not leave the library carrying him and our assorted bags while he was tantrumming—and we had to get out of here. So, praying no one in this library knew me, I took his jacket and tied it around his arms and torso like a straitjacket, grasped the knot tightly in one hand, held our things in the other, and dragged him out of the library like a trussed turkey—while everyone watched us.

Finally, we made our way out the doors and onto the sidewalk. Exhausted and desperately needing to regroup, I sat both of us down on the curb and looked at Oakley. The fresh air had stilled him. He was no longer screaming; he had moved on and was blissfully watching the cars pass by. "Oakley, you can't do that. It makes Mama so sad."

"You proud of me?" asked Oakley.

"No, Oakley, I am angry that you ran away and screamed in the library."

"Don't be angry. Be proud!" Oakley grinned wildly, and his eyes shone. It was obvious that he didn't get it. He thought that we had just played a romping game of chase. He was only angry because he had lost. Once outside and calm, he sparkled.

I groaned. How could I love this little nut so much? It was another trip to the library, another *year* off my life.

Now, at sixteen, he bikes on six-foot-tall unicycles, does backflips, juggles, and still laughs with a maniacal glee. He is still the same nut he was at three, and he still doesn't do well keeping his bum on the floor. But here in the desert? I couldn't have a better partner.

When we finally arrive at Hells Canyon, we find that instead of the craggy, desolate pit we were expecting with a name like that, there is again an oasis. The Copperfield Campground is brilliant green and stands in the armpit of an oxbow of the Snake River. The campground is filled with fly fisherman, birders, motorcyclists, and families all using the area to escape the oppressive summer heat. It is jarring to see these vacationers so far into the wild, unforgiving country, but then again, they are joined by deer, trout, coyotes, and countless other animals with the same idea. Seems that's the way the desert goes. Everything and everybody clusters around water holes where life abounds.

We immediately go jump in the river. Oakley insists on cannon-balling off tall precipices into the deepest sections, reliving the scene from Belknap Springs, while I wallow in the shallows, massaging my knees. We swim in our bike shorts to wash the sweat and stink from them, and soon enough we are approached by some curious onlookers.

"Where are you folks coming from?" asks a man sharing our swimming hole.

"The Oregon Coast. We are headed to Virginia," spouts Oakley.

"No kidding!" Before we know it, we are surrounded by a gaggle of this man's four children, his wife, and a handful of other campers.

"Where are you staying?" asks one.

"How far do you go in a day?" asks another.

"What do you carry? What do you eat?" asks a third.

We tell them all they want to know and probably more. Oakley and I bask in their attention. When the questions die down, the man speaks up again. "You know, I truck. It is really hard to see bikes out there. It is really dangerous for you and for me. I don't want to kill anybody! I am afraid for both of us."

I do understand. Trucking is this man's livelihood and our galli-vanting across the country, sharing the road, makes it all the more stressful. For the first time, I feel a little guilty that we have put them in a tight spot rather than the other way around.

"I am sorry. We try to stay way over."

"I have seen some bikers using these." He holds up two brightly colored swim noodles—one purple, one red—that he has been floating with. "We are leaving tomorrow and won't be using these anymore. If you attach them to your rear bike rack, you will be more visible to drivers and give us a bigger target to miss. It would ease my mind."

We accept the gifts, and the next morning before the sun rises, we fasten them onto the backs of our bikes and pedal even deeper into the canyon. There they will remain for the entirety of our trip, sparking endless questions, keeping us a modicum safer, and reminding us every day of all the people rooting for us.

Lessons the Desert Has Taught Us:

1. Nobody likes anyone when biking up passes at over 4,000 feet when there is no shade, it is over 90 degrees, and it is the end of a long day. This is not a character flaw. It is normal.

2. Desert sunrises are the most beautiful in the world. And the most silent.

3. One should not race down the far side of a pass with so much glee that one doesn't notice the gravel on a curve when traveling twenty-four miles an hour. One will crash. It will hurt.

4. Oakley is wonderful in a crisis. He will bring you gauze and Neosporin and offer you sympathy and support. He will also not let you forget—ever—that you dropped the f-bomb repeatedly. He will gain much pleasure from it.

5. There is nothing sweeter than descending into a place called Hell's Canyon, full of worry about the forecasted 110-degree tempera-tures and the certainty of heatstroke, and finding instead an oasis

of green and cool on the banks of the Snake River—one with swimming holes, soft grass, deep shade, and all the smart local people (and animals) enjoying a long respite from the canyon's unrelenting simmering August heat.

6. The space in the desert sky and land is humbling in its size. It can cause vertigo.

7. Bushes seem to grow from rocks. Turkeys jog down highways, high-stepping to keep their feet cool. Coyotes chortling at night will command your full attention. Hawks make a cry that is just like in the movies. Life can happen anywhere.

8. Bodies do get stronger every day. It is amazing to watch it happen to skinny sixteen-year-olds and chubby fifty-year-olds.

9. Skinny sixteen-year-olds biking over passes in the desert need more food than one can imagine. Food becomes the focus of every hour, every day. All rules about junk food and soda need to end.

10. We are entirely capable of this and make a good team.

We climb up out of the canyon, kiss the green, cool, forgiving mountains above, and then descend again to the Salmon River. The river cuts through a treeless valley that collects the sun's heat from every angle and stores it in its barren rocks. It then radiates it back and forth between its rocky walls, creating a veritable solar furnace for those unlucky enough not to be frolicking in the tumbling cool waves. As we pedal, I find my temperature yet again rising to unhealthy levels. I call to Oakley for frequent stops, but he grows frustrated because there isn't always shade to rest under. Oakley doesn't have any fat on him. When he gets hot, he sweats; he cools easy. I have plenty of juicy segments around my middle, and they insulate me far too well. When I get hot, I stay hot. Today they make me feel like I am riding in a snowsuit under the full desert sun. "Oakley," I call again. "Wait."

He groans. "Mom, let's just get there." We have been crawling up one canyon and down into the next in an area where the Snake and Salmon River have cut through the earth, creating what is equivalent to an upside-down mountain range in elevation change. We are both exhausted.

"Oakley, I am getting too hot."

"You are fine. Come on." He takes a swig from his water bottle, and I can see the sweat droplets immediately burst forth on his arms and brow. His body is working like a water filter—evaporative cooling in action. As we continue, I zone in on his back and watch his muscles grow taut again and again as he pulls himself up every incline. All parts of his body are engaged. He is a machine. I try to match his pace and focus on keeping him near, but soon he has outdistanced me.

"Oakley," I call again, but suddenly my voice sounds feeble. I feel a weakness wash through me. I reach up and touch my cheek. It is dry and papery. My vision swims. "Oakley," I call again. But he is too far now. I see him cresting a hill in the distance. He has no idea that I am dangerously close to succumbing to heat exhaustion. I reach for my whistle.

A warble pierces the air. Oakley hears it and stops. He turns and sees me slumped on the shoulder of the road. For the first time, these whistles that we have carried around for the last three weeks are serving their purpose. For the second time in a week, Oakley is going to have to save me. Slowly, I stagger up the hill toward him, feeling the air enveloping my body like hot sand. My head is throbbing, and I feel like I might be sick any moment. He looks down at me from above and calls that there is a place called Hooters up ahead where we can stop.

Hooters? Out here? Me and my sixteen-year-old son at a gentleman's club? I don't care; I just need cool. Girls in tight T-shirts might be a welcome distraction from this misery. When I finally reach him, I see that Hooters out here in the Idaho desert wilderness is not the franchise involving women in accentuating T-shirts, but rather a café with an owl motif. I admit that I am mildly disappointed. I get as far as the front door and then need to lie down on a bench outside because I think I might throw up. Oakley looks at me with concern. He crosses his arms and waits. And thinks.

After a few minutes, during which I simultaneously lie still yet orbit the sun, I hear his voice cut into my consciousness: "How about a coke?"

I slit my eyes open. "That sounds like a good idea."

I feel sweat returning to my brow and know this is a good sign. I stand and lurch after him. As he opens the door, cool air floods out from an overeager air conditioner. There is nobody in here except the soda fountain attendant, an ancient woman sitting in the corner, and owls. Hundreds of owls. Ceramic owls, wooden owls, stuffed owls, and sculpted owls. Is this a dream? We belly up to the bar and order two cokes. Slowly, I regain my senses and notice our reflection in the mirror behind the counter.

I see a poor kid looking at his mother nervously. She is covered in bike grease and crystallized salt. Her hand is bandaged with a roll of blackened first aid tape. Her legs are all akimbo, and her hair stands out in sweat-encrusted tufts from her head like a broom that has seen better days. She seems addled. "Oakley, looks like this is a two-soda day." And much to his delight, it is.

Once I have recovered a modicum of my composure, we head two more miles up the road to White Bird, Idaho, population ninety-one. It is 99 degrees, and the next feature on our journey is a 4,500-foot desert pass. No, thank you. We are told to sleep in the town square, a little fifty-foot square of grass surrounded by asphalt—new asphalt that is being applied and steamrollered today. The heat and noxious smell come off it in nauseating waves. We stumble into a bar called the Silver Dollar Café to get a little sustenance, as it is the only establishment in town, and we need our spirits lifted by something more than peanut butter.

As I open the door to this tavern, five patrons turn in their seats and squint at the light and heat coming in from behind us. It is dark and smoky and definitely not a family establishment. There Oakley and I stand in our tight biking shorts and neon yellow shirts and whistles. There is a very pregnant pause.

"How old is that kid?" asks the tired-eyed bartender.

"Sixteen. We just want something to eat."

"He can't be in here."

We turn to leave, shoulders slumped, envisioning the hot night and our unappealing peanut butter tacos, feeling and looking bereft, when a question beckons us back.

"Do you like meat lovers pizza?" the bartender asks haltingly.

Anybody who knows me knows that I am a die-hard vegetarian and have not eaten meat since I was twelve years old. I have also raised my children as vegetarians. I hesitate. Oakley looks at me with a pleading expression.

"We do, Mom. Just this once, we do."

"Do you have plain cheese?" I stammer.

"What?" asks the bartender.

Oakley's whole body begs. He is so skinny. We have been working so hard. It is so hot, and our options seem unpalatable.

"Yes, we do," I respond. I can feel a jolt of electricity run through Oakley.

"We could hide you in the back room if you want, and I could heat you up a Tony's frozen pizza in the toaster oven."

"That would be great," I respond. We dutifully follow that kind man to a storage room of sorts and wait quietly for twenty minutes, glad just to be out of the sun. We play pool on a dusty table and find a lonely dartboard with bent darts to keep us occupied.

When the pizza is ready, the bartender brings it to us with a flourish. He has a pronounced limp and shaggy black hair that he sweeps to the side as he places it on the small table before us. "I put some extra cheese on it for you since you didn't seem big on the meat idea." We devour it. Then we order another. He charges us five dollars a pizza. We are so content. I pick off the sausages and pepperoni and give them to Oakley.

We leave White Bird at 4:30 in the morning, ready to tackle yet another pass before the sun's full strength hits us. The original route over the pass has been replaced by a busy interstate highway, so, blissfully, we get to ascend on an abandoned road. There are no vehicles, no people, no industry. Just switchbacks, snaking back and forth, up and up through the predawn desert.

As we leave the town, we match the silence all around us with our own silence and just listen acutely for the sounds of wildlife waking up around us. First come the birds—the first tentative calls, the replies, and then a swelling chorus. Then come the lowing of the cows, calling for each other and for breakfast. And then come the coyotes. We hear them in the ravine that cuts up the mountainside below us. Their chatter echoes from wall to wall and creates the illusion that there are hundreds surrounding us. We stop often and peer into the shadowy valley, trying to glimpse them. Suddenly Oakley shouts in a hoarse whisper, "Look there, there! They are chasing a baby deer!"

And they are. A deer clambers up out of the ravine with three coyotes on its tail. They are hunched, yet striding swiftly and stealthily. They don't make a sound. The howls are coming from a gully, bouncing around and creating a distracting cacophony that I am sure is purposely intended to confuse the deer. The deer takes off at a run, bounding over chaparral, and the coyotes take up a more earnest chase. Suddenly, the others who had been calling erupt out of the ravine and join the pursuit. They run across the valley, and Oakley and I stand staring in awe at this wildlife theater unfolding before us. We watch until the deer gets away.

Oakley notices a cherry tree beside us. "Want a cherry?" he asks and hands me a handful. And we stand there, watching the sun come up, eating cherries until our lips are stained red.

We have now completed one thousand miles of our bicycle tour. Every day we encounter new and exciting adventures that are testing us in a myriad of ways, but also rewarding us with beautiful sights, interesting people, and growing strength. It has become a running joke between Oakley and me that we have not yet come upon a cyclops or the land of the lotus-eaters, but we know they are out here, and we won't be surprised. They would fit right in. It feels like we are participating in the *Odyssey*, but I am no Odysseus, and I can't help but wonder who is saving who on this quest.

Oakley's Two Cents

The Desert

This week we were in what I call HELL. That is actually also what the name of the area is. We went up and over passes that were straight up and all switchbacks. One day, we were going down a pass, and we were turning onto a gravel road and my mom bit it, HARD, and there was blood, like, a LOT of blood. She is okay now though.

Yesterday, we went through a place called Hells Canyon. We started on one side of the Oregon border, up above the canyon in Baker City. We woke up at 5:30 in the morning and had to cross the border into Idaho because we had to get across before the sun got too hot. The border is the Snake River, and it can get up to 110 degrees this time of year.

The day was so hot when we were there that it is no wonder it is called Hells Canyon. By the time we climbed up and out of it, we were exhausted. Luckily there was a town (Cambridge, Idaho) with a campground that had natural hot springs and a pool. Today was not that bad of a day. My mom let us sleep in for once, but that made it a very slow day. The ride was a gradual UP, UP, UP, forty-eight miles of UP. You have no idea how sick of hills and mountains we are. It's crazy. We call them all "hells" instead of hills. Tomorrow we are going to climb a hill, or pass, called White Bird. It is crazy huge. My mom misread it and thought it was called White Fang because she was so scared of it. I hope there are not more accidents, and I hope there are no more hills (after the Rockies, of course).

Those Who Come Before

August 23-29, 2019

Montana

I am a fool. Who buys a navy-blue rain suit for her knuckleheaded teenage son to wear on a bike trip across the country? Who thinks, *I know! I will dress him in an outfit that nearly camouflages him against the dark pine forests we will cycle through, one he can wear when visibility is reduced, the road is slick, and there is no shoulder. How about putting him on a heavily traveled truck route, complete with hairpin switchbacks and no shoulder?* I do. A fool.

As we climb up and over Lolo Pass and head into Montana, I am filled with anxiety. The rain is coming down in torrents, and Oakley and I are pressed between guardrails and eighteen-wheelers that are struggling to stay on the narrow road even without the added obstacle of two poorly equipped cyclists. I am glad we have our little swim noodles strapped to the back of our bikes, but they seem miniscule compared to these monster-like vehicles coming up behind us.

We have developed a fear of trucks that is similar to that found in a predator-prey relationship. I have nothing against truckers; they are working hard, and I firmly believe that no one wants to kill us. But when we hear a trucker bearing down on us from behind, and I am screaming to Oakley to get out of the road, or to pedal harder to get to the safety of the other side of a tight spot, it feels very similar to what I imagine fleeing with young from a pterodactyl might feel like.

There is nowhere to get out of the way and rest where we can be dry. When we do stop to take a breath, Oakley begins violently shivering. This is so stupid. I ply him with soggy granola bars and peanut butter crackers to keep his calories up so that his skinny body has fuel to burn. This is where my fat is an asset.

Today it is me saying, "We have to keep going."

Finally, we break through the rain clouds and arrive at the top of Lolo Pass. There is a clearing at the top of the pass with a stream running through it that feeds the Lochsa River. Shoulder-high grasses sway in the high mountain air. It is not hard to squint and see all the others that have come before. It may be cheesy, but Oakley and I can't help but feel like we are participants in a long history of past travelers who, I am sure, were even more excited to have made it to the downhill than we are.

This pass has been used to cross this range since the beginning of time by creatures of all sorts: The Nez Perce used it in the eighteenth century to cross between the Weippe Prairie in Idaho and the Bitterroot Valley in Montana. Lewis and Clark crossed it in the early 1800s. Countless unnamed trappers and traders have used it as they chased elk and buffalo from range to range. Arriving at this quiet clearing must have filled all with a similar sense of relief. The air seems to hold it. Now, all we have to do is go down to the long broad plains of Montana.

As we descend, feeling all righteous and poetic, we are passed by a Corvette, then another, then, much to Oakley's delight, nearly nine hundred, all heading off to a Corvette convention. How times change. Crazy world.

We pull into the Shady Spruce Hostel in Missoula, Montana. We have made it! Here we will take a much-needed day off and a shower. Let me just say that getting clean has become an incredibly important part of our day. We seek showers everywhere we go, and if we can't find one, we swim in our clothes. Oakley stinks to high heaven, and I am sure that I do too. Out here though, it is more than that. Being constantly this dirty seems like a health risk. The sweat and bike grease and grime that builds up under our nails and around our toes creates an ecosystem unto itself, let alone the sweat that collects in bike shorts and under jog bras. It isn't for the faint of heart. I often won't pay for a bed, but I will pay for a shower.

After that, we will check in with the TransAmerica Trail Adventure

Cycling headquarters. This place is a known spot for cross-country cyclists to recharge—over one thousand cyclists check in here on their way across the United States each year—and we are excited to sign in and bask in the glow of comradery. We have also been promised free ice cream on our visit and have biked ten miles out of our way to be given this prize. Oakley and I take turns fantasizing about the celebratory ice cream sundaes that are about to grace our palates. After a night involving showers, copious amounts of Mexican food, and movies, we stroll over to the headquarters with our heads held high.

It is a Saturday, and the building seems deserted. We pull open the door and find two bereft-looking employees who look like they would certainly rather be biking then stuck inside this office. The air is hot and stale.

"Hi, we are, um, biking across the country?" I mumble.

"Oh, great. Yeah, let's get your picture." The man unwinds himself from his desk and gets his Polaroid. We pose awkwardly against the wall. It somehow feels like a mug shot. He hands us our picture and a sticky note. "Just write your names and where you are from and stick it on the wall there." We look to where he gestures and see a wall covered in hot-pink and neon-green sticky notes with assorted bikers' photos. We take a closer look. It is somewhat interesting, as you can see that TransAmerica cyclists are comprised of people of all ages, races, and ethnicities. There are tandem bikers, violin-playing bikers, and costumed bikers. We stick our picture on the wall next to the rest of them. It is instantly lost in the sea.

"How many bikers have come through this year?"

"Oh, I don't know. A lot. They don't always go the whole way. You are late, you know? You probably won't see any out there. I hope you make it over the Rockies before the snow flies. You guys are cutting it close, and it could be a mess."

Oakley glares at me. We stand awkwardly for another few moments, but there isn't much more to say.

"Would you like a tour of the building?" he asks.

Oakley shakes his head at me and mouths, "Ice cream."

"Um, sure, but this guy here is really excited about that free ice cream?" I ask hopefully.

"Oh, yeah, help yourself." He walks over to a freezer in the corner of the room and takes out two freezer-burned boxes of popsicles, lime and coconut. Again, Oakley glares at me as if this is my fault, as if I planned this.

"Thanks so much," I say. We take our popsicles, and I nudge Oakley in an encouraging, "be friendly" way.

"Yeah, thanks," he mumbles, and off we go, a little less high in our socks. Strolling through the downtown of Missoula, we discover a music festival underway, so we sit and listen and suck on our pitiful popsicles.

"Oakley, we are pretty cool, you know."

"Yeah, I know."

Oakley and I are finishing up another long day in the hot desert sun in Darby, Montana, when my spokes break again. Pop! Pop!

What the heck? I can't take much more of this. I feel my frustration getting the best of me. How are we ever going to make it across the country if my bicycle keeps self-destructing? We are twenty miles beyond the nearest town, and I can't imagine biking back there. Ahead of us lies another high pass and miles upon miles of Montana wilderness. My hand still hurts from the embedded gravel, my heart hurts with homesickness, and I am sick to death of Oakley. I am out of ideas and feel short on gumption. "What are we going to do, Oakley?" I ask rhetorically, sitting on a guardrail, my head in my hands and sweat running down my chin.

"Send me home?" he responds, equally worn out.

And the tears come. I swallow hard, wipe my eyes with my greasy, oily fingers, and decide to ignore him. I walk to the side of the road and stick out my thumb.

"We are hitchhiking? No way!" It is obvious that Oakley can't believe that his own mother is doing something so reckless. It puts a spring in his step.

It doesn't take long before a logger picks us up in his pickup truck. He drives us all the way back to the town of Hamilton, where there is a bike store. Driving along, squished together in the front seat of the cab, the logger must sense that we are a little downhearted because he begins to give us a little inspirational speech. Maybe it's the patina of tears and bike grease ringing my eyes like I'm a down-on-her-luck raccoon.

"You two can't forget that you are choosing to do this. You guys are so lucky, and you obviously make a good team. You could catch a flight home today if you wanted," he reminds us, "but you're here because you want to be here. Both of you."

We both acknowledge the truth in this. When he drops us off at the bike shop, Oakley apologizes for his attitude. It is the first time he has been able to say he is choosing this. He is on this adventure not because I am making him, but rather because it is a challenge of his choosing. He can pretend that I am making him, but there is far more strength in realizing that he is making himself. That is what big boys do.

We fix my bike—in fact, we get a whole new rear wheel—before we head out again. The bike store owner tells me that the bike has a few kinks to work out from being reassembled in an incorrect way. This is the third time I have heard this.

In the morning, we carry on toward Wisdom, Montana. We cross the Continental Divide for the first time as we cycle by mountain goats and marmosets. We circle around the site of the Battle of Little Bighorn, also known as Custer's Last Stand, in which ten thousand Lakota Sioux and Cheyenne warriors were told of an impending attack and stood together to defeat Custer in 1876. Within five years almost all Native Americans would be confined to reservations.

Sagebrush covers the land from horizon to horizon; the color is indescribable. It is chartreuse and lavender, opal and magenta, all layered atop of each other. Is there a name for that? The light is fading from the biggest sky I have ever seen just as we swoop into town, though perhaps Wisdom would be more aptly described as a crossroads. It is comprised of maybe ten buildings and has a population of ninety-one. There is one small market, one café, a tack shop, a farm store, and a bar. Our kind of town.

We hurriedly set up our tent right outside the town and run to find something to eat before the last shop closes for the night. We sidle up to the appropriately named Antlers Saloon to see about some dinner, exhausted after a long day and ready for something more than camp food.

Inside we are welcomed by animal trophies of all varieties: deer, bear, elk, buffalo, moose, and antelope adorn every wall and look down at us with somber expressions. We are the only patrons. The bartender welcomes us heartily and announces that tonight she is making her special homemade pizza. That sounds perfect. As we sit waiting, as silent and still as all the stuffed wildlife around us, speechless with hunger, one by one the locals begin to appear. It seems that the whole town knows about pizza night. The bar transforms from something funereal to something more akin to a festival; a little blond boy climbs onto one of the bar stools and spins about. His sister takes a seat in the corner, her nose deep inside a thick book. Some other children use racks on the wall as a climbing apparatus. Ranchers come in worn and dirty. A farmer with bib overalls leans against the old-school jukebox. To complete the impromptu party, a little dog walks in through the café's open door and pees on the floor. Everyone just laughs about the establishment's open-door policy. Then out come the pizzas, with golden crusts and bubbling cheese. They are rapidly devoured by all. Seconds are served, and thirds. Oakley and I are in heaven.

Later, walking back at twilight to the old paddock where we are camping for free, we listen to coyotes yodeling and cows lowing as they bed down under the star-filled night. We pass deer and raccoons drinking from a meandering creek that runs next to the road. A family of ospreys gets in a calling match with Oakley. They return his shrill whistles again and again. The temperature that August night drops well below freezing, and the stars coat the sky with what look like shards of ice. We wake to frozen water bottles and a frosted tent. I think I know why this place is called Wisdom.

February 20, 2019

Sharon sat on my counseling couch. She was a woman in her forties with two teenage children and an uninspiring marriage. "I am just so bored," she said. "I mean, is this life? Is this all there is to it? I just work and take care of my children until I am old, and then I die? I am grateful for all I have, really, I am, it's just that all I ever do is get to the next day. You know?"

I did know. In my counseling practice, I work with clients to figure out what their values are and make sure that they are living a life that is in line with them. It doesn't matter what their mental health diagnosis is or what their values are—just that they keep their headlights on them so they don't get lost.

Often I start out with an exploration of values. Is it wealth you want, or success? How about respect or family? The list goes on and on. Pick your top ten. Now, how much attention are you giving each of these?

Sharon picked responsibility and knowledge and family. She had the family thing covered, and she loved and cared for her children very well. But what about respect and knowledge? "I used to love being in school, but I got so busy," she said.

"Busy with what?"

"Oh, you know, I waste time. Besides, I am too old now." But if this was what she valued, if this was what was important to her, then she needed to do it or she would be perpetually dissatisfied. I told her this.

"I would feel dumb in class."

"Maybe, but is what people think of you more or less important to you than knowledge? You said before that you didn't care what others think of you."

"I would feel so awkward. It would be uncomfortable."

Sharon was a runner, and I brought this up. "You run. That is uncomfortable, I am sure. I bet your legs get really uncomfortable. Especially your thighs! Seems like you are willing to get uncomfortable to get in shape."

"That is different. I am not anxious when I run."

I wondered out loud why the discomfort borne from anxiety got more credit. Seemed to me that discomfort was just discomfort. I practiced doing uncomfortable things with Sharon. We held our breath until our lungs were fit to burst. We tried to touch our toes. I gave her the homework of making an uncomfortable phone call. We practiced getting comfortable with being uncomfortable.

"Okay, this doesn't mean you sign up to get your master's degree tomorrow. Just like you don't sign up for a marathon when you are just walking around the block. But you take a step. You let yourself feel a little anxious. You look at it and say, 'There it is. There is that uncomfortable feeling,' and then, if what you are doing is in line with your values, you keep going, just like when your legs ache on a hill."

Sharon did indeed do this. She began with an online art class, and then took a writing class. She became more aware of making decisions based her values about how she spent her time. She kept her headlights pointed there, and it helped. Her anxiety and depression symptoms decreased, and her self-confidence increased. It isn't a miracle cure, and there are coping skills to help navigate anxious or depressing feelings, just like there are stretches for running, but at least she had a road map.

Some of my top values are family, the outdoors, and celebrating all that life has to offer. Oakley's values are physical fitness, adventure, and family. This bike trip is like my magnum opus.

Another day, another pass, another flat tire! Now I am losing my mind. We careen from joy to despair in minutes! I flip my bike over after taking off all the carefully packed gear and begin to try to wrestle the tire off the wheel. There is no one around, just enormous crickets lurching and jumping in a cannibalistic frenzy. Some of them are as big as our thumbs. My mood is sour. Oakley's is worse.

"Oakley, help me."

"No, you do it."

"My hand hurts from the gravel in it."

"It's fine."

"Oakley!"

He grumpily approaches my bike, removes the tire, and replaces the tube. We flip the bike right side up, reload the gear, and get back on our saddles. Within one quarter mile it is flat again. I have no more tubes, and my patch kit has been used up. Tears spring to my eyes. The sun beats down without a tree or cloud in sight, and we are low on water. Nothing is working out. I guess it is time to hitch again. Again, Oakley loves it. I stew.

It isn't easy to get a ride with two bicycles and all the assorted gear. Car after car passes us, and we make all sorts of disparaging remarks about people who are seemingly happy to leave us out here to die by rabid coyote. Finally, I see a truck coming down a dirt road, and before he has a chance to turn onto the highway, I race to his window and rap on it.

"Hi there! Sorry to bother you, but we could really use some help." The old man behind the wheel just stares at me, seeming to not comprehend a word I am saying. "I have a flat tire that I can't fix. We have no water. Could you drive us to town?" Still he stares and seems to weigh his options. I suppose he realizes he can't in good faith leave us out here with the buzzards. Wordlessly, he opens the door and gets out.

He gestures to the back of the truck and mumbles, "Load them up."

We don't miss a second and toss everything into the bed as quickly as possible before he changes his mind. Then we squeeze into the small cab with him and sit, pressing our stinky, sweaty selves shoulder to shoulder. I practically feel like we are kidnapping him. Finally, he begins to speak.

"I lost my dog this morning. He was hit, right out here, by a truck. Didn't even stop. He is in the back now; I am taking him to the transfer station."

Oakley and I look at each other, wide-eyed. That was the lumpy black plastic trash bag that we threw all our gear on top of!

"I loved that dog. He was only a pup. Two." He wipes away tears from his rheumy eyes. "I never trained her not to chase cars. I should have."

I begin trying to console him, but what can I say? We ask him questions about his life out here in this foreign world of prickly pear and sand. Thirty miles later he has become animated and tells us all about life on his ranch and moving to town and his grandchildren. When he finally drops us off in the town of Dillon, he is smiling. "You two be careful, okay? Oh crap, I forgot about the dog! Now the transfer station is closed. I will have to go tomorrow." He chuckles, and off he drives.

Now we sit on the sidewalk, waiting outside a home where he told us a man that used to fix bikes lives. There are no bike shops in town, so this seems like our best option. Neighborhood cats circle around us, covering our sweaty knees and hands with their fur while we come to the conclusion that we would rather have countless flats than a dead beloved pet. Finally, Oakley says, "Mom, nobody is coming."

"Somebody will come."

"You don't know that."

"They will."

"Why are you saying that? You have no idea!"

"Because they always come, Oakley. I am starting to just believe that. It will work out."

An hour later, when the homeowner comes home and sees us sitting outside his house, he seems to assess our situation at a glance and launches into action. "Need help? Bring them in here, and I will see what I can do. Are you on the trail?" He is a ponytail-wearing professor at the local university and is in charge of their outdoor education program. He is no stranger to outdoor gear malfunctions.

We push my bike into his garage, which is scattered with every bike part imaginable, and as we watch, he expertly whips off the tire, sands down the rim in case there is a metal burr creating the problem, covers the inner rim in slick protective tape, and remounts it all. Then he grabs Oakley's bike, throws it up on the stand, tightens this loose bolt and that crooked pedal, and hands it back with a flourish. "You're good to go. That is on the house. They are in perfect shape now. Good luck out there."

We officially have our bicycles—and our faith in humanity—restored.

Virginia City, town of wooden sidewalks, swinging saloon doors, and gold mines set on the side of a mountain. Stories of vigilantes, gunslingers, and posses feel like today's news here. History is still at your fingertips in these regions because so little has changed. Perhaps it is because of the lawless, wild feeling in these little western towns. But Oakley and I also begin to confront his own anarchical behavior.

First, he miraculously finds a twenty-dollar bill in the sand on the side of the road, right after mine had gone missing. Then I find his bags littered with food wrappers from food that I have been saving for a later time. And then there's the ring.

We are in a little gem shop on the side of the road in Virginia City. I have been waylaid by the owner, listening to her preach about the "do-good, head-in-the-sand liberals that populate the East Coast and come here for vacation with their high-faluting leftist beliefs," while Oakley fondles boxes of geodes, gems, and knickknacks. I see him holding a mood ring in his hand. My skin prickles.

The shop owner keeps ranting. "Come here talking about Obama this and environment that when they have no idea! They are all so high and mighty. You know, they are the ones that steal and ruin things. I swear." My eyes are on Oakley and his crafty fingers. We need to get out of here.

"Hey, Oakley, we should get to the campground before it gets dark!" I call.

Oakley gives a quick bob of his head and scurries to the door.

"Thanks so much. Have a great day!" I say as airily as I can muster, being that she just verbally slaughtered me and my people.

Oakley and I grab our bikes and head out to set up our tent. I feel uncomfortable, and I am not sure why. We stop to check the map, and that is when it happens.

"Mom, look what I found." He is bent over his bike, staring at the sand. I don't want to ask. I study the maps instead.

"Mom, look!" And he holds up his prize, a purple dime-store mood ring.

"Oh, Oakley."

"What? Do you think I stole this?"

"I don't know."

"Mom! I didn't! You are so annoying! I found it." He puts it on his finger, and it fits perfectly. What are the chances? Now he is fuming at my suspicion. I don't know. Will I ever know?

After a long day of riding, we finally reach the border of Montana. Oakley has been racing me today and seems especially exhausted. When he climbs off his bike, he walks like a cowboy who's spent too long in the saddle. It is time to stretch out and rest. We are planning to camp at Earthquake Lake, without much thought about what the name might connotate. When we arrive, we are struck by the eeriness of the area.

At the local visitor's center, we learn that this was the setting of a huge landslide caused by an earthquake in 1970. The quake took place in the height of the summer season and caused half a mountain to slide down into a valley, blocking a river and causing a surge of water to fill in behind it. The water and the rubble caused the deaths of forty-nine people who had been vacationing in the spot. Many were never found and are still thought to be buried under thousands of tons of rock and debris. Needless to say, we are rattled as we pull into our campsite and begin setting up our tent in the wake of such a tragedy.

Quietly, I begin making dinner while Oakley works on creating a cozy sleeping area for us. We are soon joined by the campground host. As he wobbles off of his ATV, it is obvious that he is right sick of his job, and the summer of tending to tourists has worn him out. He doesn't smile, and barely makes eye contact.

"Did you pay?" is his greeting.

"Hello, yes, I did. I put it in the fee station."

"Fine, be careful of the bears." And he turns to leave.

"Um, just so you know, I ran out of cash and only put sixteen dollars in the slot. I know the price is twenty, but it is all I had. I didn't realize forest service campgrounds were so expensive! Sorry." I am sorry, but also annoyed at the price of camping, and when you are biking through the wilderness and you run out of money, what can you do?

He spins on his heel. "Do you know how irresponsible that is?"

"Yes, I am sorry," I stammer again, shocked that it is such a big deal.

"You can't stay here."

"I really am sorry. I thought I had more. We have nowhere else to go. It is just me and my son on bikes, and it will be dark soon."

"Should have thought of that before. Pack it up."

Oakley looks at me with horror. We cycled sixty-five miles today, and there is only about twenty minutes of light left in the sky. There are no streetlights out here, just mile after mile of country road snaking through the thick forest.

"I really can't. It wouldn't be safe."

"Not my problem." This poor man has the weight of the world on him for four dollars!

"Is there an ATM anywhere near here?" I begin rifling through my bags, furiously searching for any crumpled wet bill, but I find none.

"Nope, closest one is ten miles down the road, if they are open, which"—he looks at his watch—"they are not." Again, Oakley looks at me with pleading eyes.

I begin to plead myself. "If you follow us there in the morning in your car, I will give you the difference. I promise. I am so sorry."

"You have no business being out here so woefully unprepared. It is people like you that ruin it for everyone. You give me no choice. Fine, I will be here at 6:00 a.m. tomorrow morning. You better be up and ready to go." And off he stomps.

Oakley is furious. "Mom, he is an idiot! I hope a bear attacks him! What is his problem? Let's just get out of here in the morning before he comes."

"No, Oakley, he needs some niceness."

"No, he doesn't!" This is the first time we have been met with anything

128

but kindness out on the trail. I can only guess that the campground host has had a long summer of tourist abuse and it has unhinged him.

The next morning, after a fitful sleep filled with fears of both bears and missing our wake-up call, we make our way ten miles down the road to a small café with an ATM. While the campground host waits with a harassed frown, I take out a twenty and bring it back to him. He takes it gruffly and opens his wallet to give us change.

"You can keep it." I say.

"Wait now, you already paid sixteen."

"That is okay, wouldn't want to make a big deal out of a few dollars. Take yourself out to breakfast."

"Oh no, that wouldn't be right." He fumbles to give us the money, and his face softens contritely.

We quickly hop aboard our bikes and pedal away. "That is how to kill with kindness," I whisper to Oakley as the host calls from behind us, "Hey, be safe! Have a really good trip. Good luck! Get some bear spray!"

"Thank you," Oakley calls back, and I can see his body ignite with positive energy. He laughs. "That poor guy!"

Oakley's Two Cents

So Many Switchbacks!

It is week four, and personally, I think we have completed the hardest part of our trip. We have ridden over huge passes and gone over never-ending hills. We have been camping in town parks under sprinklers that turn on in the middle of the night and drive you crazy.

A couple days ago we stayed in a little desert town called White Bird. It was the real Wild West. We got up early before the sun was up and set out to climb the deadly White Bird pass. It was thirteen miles of straight up switchbacks. I think we are getting pretty strong.

On the way up we saw coyotes and deer prowling the plains spread out below us. Once we got over the pass, the whole landscape changed from dry desert to farmlands. That seems to happen every time we cross a pass.

Yesterday, we had a long and gradual climb up the Lolo Pass to get to Missoula. On the way over we hit one thousand miles. We are making really good progress. In a week we will be in Yellowstone. I can't believe we have finished one fourth of this trip.

Can You Breathe Silence?

August 29-September 8, 2019

Wyoming

Oakley and I come crashing into West Yellowstone, Montana, under an unstable sky of cumulus clouds and fierce winds. Our first stop is the ranger station. We have been warned that Yellowstone is not great for biking. There are bears, there are bison, and there are RVs being driven down narrow roads by people who have never driven anything bigger than a Prius. With all these rumors of potential dangers, we want facts. We sashay up to the ranger counter.

"Hi there, do we really need bear spray?

"You're biking, yes. It is fifty dollars a can. Your park pass is eighty."

That is far more than we have budgeted for.

"Really? How many bear and bison attacks have there been this year?

"Well, a woman lost her dog to a bear last week, and about one person is seriously injured every year from a grizzly. Last month, a nine-year-old was attacked by a bison and thrown. She survived. She was lucky. Most of these people have cars to retreat to; you won't."

"So, to just bike through the park and buy two cans of bear spray is 180 dollars?"

"Yes. If you want to be safe."

This is not in our budget. "Let me think on it." We wander around the town, waiting for a cloudburst to pass and giving me time to decide if this advice is fear based or prudent. Seems everywhere we go, people tell us that there is something god-awful to fear: rattlesnakes, dogs, trucks, bears, storms. It is getting hard to tell which worries are truly justified and which are born from people watching too much reality television. We dart from shop to shop to hide from the rain, and I find myself idling near store counters and trying somehow to casually

131

work bear attacks into conversations while keeping one hairy eyeball on Oakley. I figure that the locals would know.

"So," I ask a sweet-looking woman in a gem shop, "do you think it is really dangerous to bike in Yellowstone without bear spray, or is that just a gimmicky tourist thing?"

"Oh no, hon, you need it. On a bike? Yes, dear. I am going to give you mine. My conscience wouldn't let me have you go without. No fooling. People die." She grabs her can of bear spray that she happens to have under the sales counter and thrusts it toward us. "I can't have a mauling on my hands." We gratefully accept it.

Later in a bike shop we are told the same thing.

"Yes, you really need bear spray if you are traveling on bikes. Also, if there are bison on the road, don't pass them. They will charge you. Wait for a car to come and then hide beside it as they pass. Keep the vehicle between you and the bison. If they stamp their feet, they are feeling ornery, so get out of there. And use bear boxes. No snacks in your tent. Don't forget the crackers you might accidently leave in your jacket pocket. They will sniff out anything."

Oakley and I look at each other with a slight panic rising, both of us knowing full well that he has a penchant for hiding his snacks in all manner of pockets and satchels. Suddenly, it feels like we are about to enter Jurassic Park. I decide that fifty dollars a can for bear spray is a mighty good investment. I hand over the cash for a second can.

During a brief respite from the rain, Oakley and I decide to go for it. We strap our spray onto the handlebars for quick access, don our rain gear, and sally forth through the gates and into the park itself. Maybe it is because the sky is dark and tangled-looking from rain clouds, maybe it is the wind, but as Oakley and I cycle into the park, we both become taut with fear. There are no tourists on the road because of the stormy weather. Who should ride in front? Who in the back? Which is more vulnerable? I think we both picture a huge behemoth erupting out of roadside foliage and devouring us headfirst. At one point, Oakley rides so close to me that he hits my rear pannier and goes careening into the bushes. As he races to collect his scattered gear, he is visibly pale and shaking.

"It's okay, Oakley. Don't panic. We are fine." He glares at me, hoping I am right, yet choking on cortisol.

We spend three days in the park. We see geysers and fumaroles, endless tourists, and starry skies. We even see a large road sign that says "STAY IN VEHICLE. GRIZZLIES IN ROAD" while ascending a hill so steep that we can only go a few panic-stricken miles an hour. But do we see one large mammal? Anything at all? No. Of course not.

Leaving Yellowstone feels like a relief from both the fear and our annoyance at all the tourists. We have grown comfortable with a little more elbow room, but every site at Yellowstone is chock-full of slowly moving, selfie-taking parades of people. It is hard to feel like you discover anything new there. We were told that if we get off the main trails, we will have the park to ourselves, but with the fear of grizzlies in our heads, we bow out.

I have never paid much attention to the Tetons, and neither has Oakley. The plan is to give them a nod as we pass by and then head on. We are anxious to make some tracks after taking some shorter days around Yellowstone, yet as we curve around the edge of Jackson Lake, suddenly, out of nowhere, the Teton Mountains rise up, cutting holes through the sky above. We are wonderstruck.

They are still wearing skirts of snow in early September, and their jagged peaks hold court over the beautiful clear lake. Oakley exclaims that the scene reminds him of a screensaver for a computer. That is high praise from a teenager. We are stopped in our tracks by the sight. Literally.

We had planned to ride upwards of sixty miles today, but we ride just another ten and pull over to camp. Neither of us can let the beauty become just a memory quite so fast. We swim in the cool, clear water of Jackson Lake and watch the sun set behind the mountains. The colors of the sky reflect off the snowy peaks and the water, and the black jagged cutouts of the mountains leave both of us speechless. Leaving is agony as the feeling that this trip is going too fast invades our thoughts again and again.

We climb Togwotee Pass, and after a twenty-five-mile ascent, we are treated to alpine meadows full of flaming red wildflowers, tall grasses, and towering rock outcroppings. It is a wilderness paradise up here. The air is thin and cool, and there are few people about. It feels like a secret. A sweet goodbye gift from this beautiful area.

Oakley's Two Cents

Things to Fear

In Yellowstone we were told that the bears are really bad this year. The ranger said it would be the best idea to buy bear spray since people have died from getting attacked by bears. If we encounter a "big ole griz," we should spray it. In case y'all don't know, Bear is my middle name, and I'm not scared of a grizzly. Actually, I'm terrified.

Other people have told us all kinds of other things to worry about. We should be careful of bison and moose. I have never heard of anyone being attacked by a moose. We were told to be aware of rattlesnakes. We have been told about hail being the size of grapefruits, lightning storms, and forty-mile-an-hour headwinds.

The landscapes that we have passed are amazing. Today we entered the Grand Tetons, and the view is something you would use for a background for a computer screen. We have passed through tiny towns (like Wisdom, which was our favorite) and Virginia City (an old gold mining town). I can imagine my life if I lived there. It might be cool.

We awake on the floor of a church in Dubois a few days later, knowing the day before us will be another test. The gift of hospitality that these churches provide cannot be understated. To occasionally sleep where we know we will be dry and safe is a balm for days of built-up tension. They also allow for an early departure. Today we will ride seventy-four miles through the Wind River Range to Lander, Wyoming. We have been told that the heat and the wind are intense in this area and that it will be bone dry. We load up with extra water and skedaddle by 6:00 a.m. to beat the heat.

The miles fly by in the morning, and we travel deeper and deeper into a land reminiscent of Mars. The soil is red and dry, and large crumbly, rocky bluffs line the roadway. From time to time, we pass a trailer with a yard lined with hubcaps or rusty half-fallen-down barbed wire. The signs of extreme poverty are everywhere. It seems hard to imagine living out here, so far from the comforts of town, when the weather is so relentless and there are so few resources.

We pass a sign on the side of the road announcing that we are entering the Wind River Range Reservation, and we are both struck by the cruelty of this. Yes, the land is beautiful, but it is hard living out here. It seems so unjust that we have only left the most inhospitable places for those that were here before us.

We pass the sight of the Sand Creek Massacre, where a sign tells of the slaughter of 184 Arapaho and Cheyenne peoples in 1864. They were butchered while they slept here after being assured by US troops that they were safe. The recorded order from the American colonel was

"Scalp them all, big and little. Nits make lice." I am truly ashamed. It is easy to imagine that there could still be encampments right over the next rise or down by the river. I feel we are still trespassing.

Oakley is struck with the horror of what humans are capable of. From horizon to horizon stretches barren land with little water and scant vegetation. "It isn't fair that this hellhole is the land that the Native Americans were given for a reservation. After what we did to them, they should get the best places."

I can't agree more.

On we travel through miles upon miles of intense heat, wind, and sun. When we finally reach Lander, we feel like dried husks. We stay in the city park, which is covered with soft verdant grass maintained with an in-ground sprinkler system and a team of maintenance workers. There are a bunch of other adventurers camping here: rock climbers, hikers, and paddlers, all outfitted with the finest gear. Everybody here is white. Oakley and I go out and eat an enormous Mexican dinner and then watch *Spider-Man* in the theater downtown before nestling down into our cozy bags, fat and happy—and very aware of how unfair it is.

A day later, it is twilight, and I am walking through the Wyoming desert alone. Oakley has chosen to stay behind and read his book. He is exhausted after another sixty-five-mile day. Today we traveled through the Wind River Reservation to Jeffrey City in southwest Wyoming. I feel the need to stretch my legs before calling it a night.

It is funny that Jeffrey City calls itself a city. It is a cluster of beaten-up trailers, a rock shop, a gas pump, and a tiny motel. We are the only guests. Usually, the towns in this area are centered around a river or some sort of moisture that creates a green oasis, but not this one. There is no water here (other than whatever feeds the park's sprinklers) and no trees, just miles of sagebrush, dry prairie grass, and rocky promontories. There used to be a bustling uranium mine, but when the mine closed, Jeffrey City became a ghost town.

Through the encroaching darkness, a few miles away from this small cluster of buildings and deep in the vast desert dusk, I can see the distant glow from the light in a lone trailer nestled under a rocky outcropping. *What are they doing out there?* I wonder. It is incredibly isolated. It must be lonely. What a different life from mine.

The wind seems to blow continually in this area—a huge nuisance as we biked today. Tonight, though, as my hair whips around my face, I welcome it. It is cool and soothing. I stroll down a sandy road that seems to lead nowhere. The sand under my flip-flops pillows my feet.

It wants to rain, and the clouds filling the sky are dropping their moisture only to have it evaporate before the rain reaches the ground. Huge curtains of rain cover the sky above me, and the clouds sag, but only a few drops make it down to tingle on my cheeks. The air is heady with the smell of sage, and it seems as though the leaves of the plants are releasing all their fragrance in hopes that it will entice the rain to try a little harder to reach them.

After Oakley's constant chatter, I embrace this moment of solitude. The quiet is a balm to a day that was filled with intensity: sweat, sun, wind, Oakley's many moods, and trucks whizzing by. I breathe in the silence.

Along the side of the road, there is a herd of antelope. The males are standing proudly with their tall black pronged antlers, looking at me quizzically and sizing up whether I am a threat. The females stand with their young, also watching, some springing away as I approach, showing me their fluffy white behinds that seem to glow in the darkening night. A fox runs across the road ten feet in front of me. His eyes catch mine for an instant, and then he is gone.

It has become truly dark, and I should head back. Oakley will worry. Before I turn around, I peer once more out at the trailer set against the rocks so far from this little town. Someone is in there. They live here and can experience this every night. I think I do understand what they are doing out here.

As I walk back, I am filled with a deep calm and a longing to have more of this in my life. The next day we might be hammered by a swirling sandstorm, winds may gust at up to sixty miles an hour, and we may be crushed by traffic on busy roads. This night, though, in this hardscrabble town, there is momentary peace in our lives, the kindness of a solitary motel keeper, and the comfort of a puzzled herd of antelope.

When I return to our meager motel, the innkeeper is standing outside our door. In her hands she holds a paper bowl filled with four clementines and a handful of cherries. "What you two are doing is amazing. I just wanted to give you something. Will you take this?" She couldn't have known what a perfect gift this was. After days and days of endless heat and eating out of convenience stores and greasy spoons, the color and the juice of that fruit is a feast for the soul. Or perhaps she does know, because when Oakley opens the door to see who I am talking to, his eyes light up like Christmas, and we immediately gobble them down while she watches.

Muddy Gap is an intersection rather than a town. The maps declare it a town, but that is because there is nothing else around, so anything deserves a name. It is a solid forty miles from the next bit of civilization, with no homes, no shops, no highway patrol. There is a gas station of sorts that sells chips, so if you are in the market for Fritos, Takis, Cheese Doodles, Lays, and soda, you are in luck. Other than that, no dice. We stop in and try to construct a lunch. Everything seems extraordinarily salty, and we feel like we would kill for an apple, or ice cream, or, God be praised, a salad. The walls are covered with graffiti, inside and out. The names of bikers and other travelers in Sharpie and colored pen cover every inch of space. It seems like a desperate monument of sorts for those who have come before us.

The man at the counter slouches dispiritedly. Seems like maybe he has seen some trouble in his time. I wonder where he commutes from and what he gets paid. It can't be enough. We grab some waffle chips and a bag of peanuts and head out, glad to be moving on.

We make it down the driveway of the gas station and begin to pedal along the highway before Oakley starts calling me. "Mom, stop!"

I am feeling anxious to make some tracks, and I shout back over my shoulder, "Come on, Oakley, I want to get out of here and find some real food!" I keep cycling, thinking he is probably just complaining about something inconsequential.

"Mom! Stop!" he calls frantically, from farther back now. "My wheel is not connected!"

He has got to be kidding. Of course it is connected. He is such an exaggerator! I am almost angry. I head back to him and find that, true enough, he is missing the axel to his front wheel. It is gone. *How is this possible?* The wheel is pinched precariously between the front forks. One bump, one pothole, one wobble, and he would been smeared across the tarmac.

"Oh my gosh, Oakley. Where is it?"

"I don't know!" he shrieks. We scurry down the highway shoulder, looking for the axel among the trash, random car parts, and scattered debris, but it is no use.

Time to hitch another ride, but prospects don't look good. There is no traffic. A car passes every fifteen minutes or so, but nobody has any room for our bikes. We are wilted from the sun's heat baking us from above and the pavement's heat radiating us from below—the proverbial heat sandwich. We are thirsty and have only our salty chips to eat. The barrenness of this land hits us. Its intensity seems cruel.

An hour passes before a truck finally pulls over. Salvation. His truck is full of hunting and camping gear, replete with two propane tanks, several bags of food, four five-gallon water containers, camping chairs, backpacks, rifles, and crossbows. How will we possibly fit? He jumps out of the truck with a broad smile.

"I couldn't in good conscience leave you out here. Get in out of the heat, and I will load your bikes." He clears a spot for us in his cab, brushing piles of cracked pistachios off the front seat for me—"I am trying to quit chewing"—and stuffs Oakley between two rifles and a crossbow in the narrow cab extension.

Once we are stowed, he sets about trying to cram our bikes and all our panniers into his heavily loaded truck bed. Once they are fastened on top of the load with ropes and bungee cords, we look very much like the Beverly Hillbillies. He tells us that he is on his way to the Rocky Mountains to hunt elk. It is an annual trip. With the elk, he feeds his family of four all winter long.

"I am not a yahoo hunter. I am really not. I just take one, and we use it all. I feel better getting our meat this way than from a feedlot. It is better for the environment too."

He is our hero.

After forty miles of air-conditioning, chattering, and looking dolefully out at the unforgiving desert, we find ourselves approaching Rawlins. He drives us to a sport hunting shop and makes sure we are in good hands. Then he plies us with twenty Gatorade packets: "You need these out here, no joke. This sun will eat you up! Be safe."

The man at the sport hunting shop has no bike parts, but he recollects that a friend who works at a local car service station really likes biking. He also loads our bikes and all our gear into a truck and shepherds us over to said station. Once we're there, a group of men encircle us and ponder where to get a bike axel. One of them says that his daughter has a bike at home she hardly ever rides, and if we would just wait a second, he will go "borrow" her axel. While we sit in the parking lot drinking Gatorade, he blitzes home and comes back carrying the axel like a trophy. I don't think that Oakley and I ever knew the world could be so kind.

Soon, after many thank-yous, we are ready to ride again. However, it is now late afternoon, and it has been a long day. Oakley and I ask these kind people where we can camp locally.

"There is a KOA in town, but you don't want to stay there. Lots of crime and drugs, plus it's ugly. You should either stay in a hotel or head out of town."

Oakley puts up a fight and wants desperately to stay in town, but after all the kindness extended to us by these people, I feel the least we can do is continue on our adventure. I think they would enjoy watching us ride into the sunset. Plus, in my mind we have cheated by getting a forty-mile ride.

"Let's go, Oakley," I call. Begrudgingly, he follows.

Little do I realize that the next sixteen miles of the trip will be the most dangerous section of the entire TransAmerica Trail. This is the only section of the trail that is routed on the shoulder of a major highway, Interstate 80. It is one of the most heavily traveled cross-country arteries, full of trucks and RVs barreling through the desert trying to make time between distant cities.

Nervously, we pedal up the ramp. The shoulder is strewn with debris, and traffic is thronging the the four-lane highway. Could this be right? We check our maps. Sure enough, this is the only way out of town. Well, if other bikers have braved it, so can we.

"Okay, Oakley, stay right behind me and way over against the guard-rail." We ease out onto the road. The gusts from the trucks push and pull us willy-nilly. I think they are as nervous as we are to see us out here. We do not belong.

"I love this!" shouts Oakley. "Biking on a highway is so fun!"

What the heck is he talking about? This is terrifying! But I know that, true to form, my little guy is a stimulation junkie, and this is nothing if not stimulating. I grip the handlebars tightly and press on. Sixteen miles—I calculate that is about an hour of travel. We can do this.

Just then, a tailwind picks up and seems to help us along. I glance over my shoulder to see where it is coming from, and there, five miles behind us, I see a black cloud galloping toward us across the sky. It is the color of soot. Lightning bolts spew, hitting the ground below at a horrifyingly regular pace. I can see that the trees are starting to lay prostrate on the ground before the storm.

You have got to be kidding me! This is too much! "Oakley, we have to get out of here!"

Oakley looks back and is also truly horrorstruck. His face whitens. There is nowhere to go except forward. There are no exits, no turning around or going back against the freeway traffic.

"Mom, this is not okay!" shouts Oakley, the thrill of highway riding gone. We begin to pedal as fast as possible. The wind grows.

"Stay with me, Oakley!" I shout again.

"I am!" he screams in return.

Just when I think that things couldn't really become more perilous, we enter road construction. Across the median, the lanes going west have been detoured to share the eastbound lanes we are on. This requires the shoulder that we are cycling on to be redesignated as a travel lane, and in a ragged heartbeat, we are now sharing the road with two-directional traffic with no shoulder in high winds. An already scary set of circumstances has become atrocious.

"Stay over!" I scream again. I don't want Oakley to bike in front of me because there isn't room for him to pass me, and even if he could, I would not be able to bear seeing his vulnerable little body wiggling nearer to and farer from the crushing tires of the trucks. We can nearly touch them as we ride.

The storm licks our backs, and the wind begins gusting with a hurricane force, picking up dust and debris and filling the sky with a yellow cloud. We pass under an overpass with a sign reading "Caution: Wind Gusts Up to 80 mph." Trucks and RVs start to sway in the wind, getting pushed closer and closer to us.

I am really scared.

Suddenly—a gift. A rest stop on our side of the highway. Relief floods us as we careen down the ramp away from the cacophony of the traffic. Cars and trucks fill the parking lot, waiting for the storm to pass. We run into the safety of the restroom pavilion and watch as the rain pelts the windows and lightning flashes all around. We consider sleeping on the floor of the bathrooms despite the signs on the walls reminding travelers that it is against the law and wonder if the police would forgive us considering the circumstances.

Then, just like that, it is over. The storm passes overhead, and we can see the smudge of its darkness blowing away across the desert toward the distant horizon. The cars in the parking lot clear out, and we do too. The trucks still blast by, only a few feet from our spindly selves. We ride the remaining six miles, still with no shoulder, hoping luck will continue to be on our side.

Finally, we leave the highway and ride the last twenty miles to Saratoga, Wyoming, on a sweet country lane. Oakley has very little to say to me. He is exhausted and enraged, terrified and empty. We pass through beautiful fields of wheat glowing like spun gold in the sliver of the setting sun that cuts through the clouds. Some of the most beautiful land we have seen, but it is lost on him. He needs a day off. We both do.

Saratoga is a beautiful small town in the high desert of Wyoming. It consists of eight cross streets, a small school, two or three restaurants, a bookstore, and some glorious natural hot springs—paradise, really. On our day off, I hit the hot springs and the ice cream parlor. Oakley seeks some independence. This time he has my blessing, much different from when we were in this exact town once before, a long, long time ago.

Oakley was four. Our family was on a summer adventure retracing the Oregon Trail. We had traveled for a week with a covered-wagon outfit across the high deserts of Wyoming to reconstruct a little history. It had been a hard but thrilling trip, and we were taking a day off in Saratoga.

"I need to go into the bookstore," said Twain. "I'll take Raven, Finn and Jonah. It's your turn with Oakley."

"I want to go to the bookstore too," I said.

"You know that we can't take Oakley in there. Come on. It will ruin it for everybody. If you take him for a walk now, I will take him later."

It was indeed my turn, and I knew he was right. Oakley just deshelved bookstores. He made everything civilized uncivilized. Just two days previous, he had locked himself in a Porta-Potty and unrolled four rolls of toilet paper—super fun, but a huge mess.

"Fine," I said sullenly and walked away down the street trailing Oakley by two feet.

We got to the end of the block and turned the corner; Oakley strode confidently just a few steps ahead. I was annoyed at his endless theatrics, but as I watched his little stomping feet and tousle of blond hair, I couldn't help but love him. It was like loving a baby raccoon. I followed closely after him, but as I turned the corner in his wake, he was gone. *What? Is he Houdini?* There was a large bay door opening into a NAPA Auto Parts storeroom, and I figured he must have ducked in there. I darted in after him. "Oakley?" I called. Rows of floor-to-ceiling shelving filled a room the size of a garage. "Oakley?"

No response. With a sinking feeling, I realized that he was playing hide-and-seek. I would never win. This was his specialty. "Oakley, come here, buddy. We aren't playing now. Want some ice cream?"

Nothing. Except for a voice from the attached shop out front: "Can I help you somehow? You can't be in here."

"I know," I said, embarrassed. "I think my son wandered in here, and I am just trying to get him out."

"He can't be in here."

"Yeah, I know. He's hiding." The man helped me look for a moment, but it soon became clear that Oakley had done the old dodge-and-weave trick and had fled while we were distracted looking behind assorted boxes.

"Must have gone down the alley. I will find him," I said brightly, feeling yet again like an incompetent parent. I looked down the alley and behind a few trashcans, then jogged back around the block, but he was nowhere. I wasn't worried yet, but I knew I needed help. I hustled back to the bookstore where I found Twain and the other children peacefully lounging on the floor and on cozy chairs reading various books.

"I lost him."

Twain rolled his eyes and sighed heavily.

"Okay," he said, and all the children got to their feet. "Let's find him."

We fanned out across the town, stopping in the few shops and restaurants that we found. We tried to be low-key so as to not draw too much attention, but when you ask a salesperson if they have seen a basically nonverbal, towheaded three-year-old wandering alone through the streets, people worry. Before we knew it, half the town had shut down, and the locals were looking with us. Ten minutes stretched to an hour and then an hour and a half. There had been road construction going on, but they too silenced their machines and joined the search. Still, I wasn't worried. Embarrassed, yes. Worried, no. This was Oakley, the runner.

Suddenly, a man came out from his house and called, "Hey, are you looking for a little kid? I just got home, and there is one sitting on my living room floor playing with my daughter's toys." You could feel a collective sigh of relief ripple through the town.

"Yep, that would be him." And when I retrieved him, he was happy as could be, grinning up at us with his sparkling blue eyes from this man's plush carpet, surrounded by toys of all varieties. I scooped him up and planted a kiss on his head.

His life was fast becoming the longest game of chase I have ever had.

Oakley's Two Cents

Best Day Off

Today we took a day off in Saratoga, Wyoming. Yesterday was so stressful because of high winds and because my front wheel fell off. I wasn't hurt, but we had to hitchhike to the nearest town for repairs. Once back on the road, we were hit by a powerful sandstorm while we were biking on the highway.

Saratoga is a cool town, though, and we went to the community gym to find people to hang out with. I met a boy named Steven. He asked if I could ride dirt bikes and ATVs at his house, and in a moment of weakness, my mother said yes.

First, we went to his house. We rode his ATV all over the hills of Saratoga, doing jumps and drifts and tearing it up. Then we had to check in with my mom. We met her at a river that is fed with hot springs and has little rocky pools on the sides. We floated down the river and into the pools. One was 118 degrees!

My mom let us disappear again, so we did. We went back to Steven's house, and while I was making a peanut butter and jelly sandwich, I looked down, and a four-foot lizard was at my feet! (An iguana.) In his backyard was also a cage full of ten two-week-old kittens. Steven locked me in with them!

After that, he took me to his grandfather's house where his dirt bikes are. His grandfather looks just like Gus McCrae from *Lonesome Dove*. We rode dirt bikes everywhere. They are not hard to figure out.

I asked Steven to get my gloves out of my bike bag, and he accidentally set off my canister of bear spray. That was exciting.

Before I left to go back to our campsite, Steven's father came home from hunting. I was standing in the front yard, and he got out of his truck with a rifle. "Get out of my yard!" he shouted. Then he smiled. He was joking.

It was the best day off ever.

Come On, Mom

September 9-16, 2019

Colorado

It is customary to check in at the sheriff's office when sleeping in the city park. It is both to help protect the town from vagrants and to give the police a way to contact you in the case of severe weather. In Walden, Colorado, it is our first stop.

Oakley is feeling ornery due to riding on a soft tire for the last sixty-some miles. I hadn't known it was soft—I had thought he was just being lazy—but when this happens, it does have its perks. I can keep up with him! We stagger up the courthouse steps and are directed by the receptionist (who also gives us peppermints from the bowl on her desk) to go down to the basement where the sheriff is conducting some business.

We go down the steps and find a closed door. I open it. Sitting there in the center of the room is a teenage boy just about Oakley's age, dressed in all prison stripes. At first it looks like a costume, and we try not to stare.

"Sorry, we were looking for the sheriff."

"I'm over here," says a warm voice, and the sheriff comes in the room holding a baby. It is only a few months old. He hands it to the teenage boy along with a bottle, and the boy wraps it tightly in his arms and begins to feed it. The father's bangs create a hood over his eyes, and he stares into the baby's eyes as it sucks in private reverie. The love he projects is intense, and we feel embarrassed to be watching.

We quickly fill out the necessary forms and hustle on our way. When we are safely out of the courthouse, the questions begin.

"Mom, what do you think he did? He seemed like such a good dad. How long do you think he will be in there?" Both of us hope that the law is lenient. That he will get another chance. That the love that boy has for his baby will carry him wherever he needs to go.

By the time we hit Colorado, we have climbed the Continental Divide six times. Still, we are wary of the big one: Hoosier Pass, elevation 11,500 feet. Have I mentioned that we live on an island on the coast where everything is at sea level?

The days leading up to this challenge are long and difficult, albeit beautiful. More green is filling into the landscape, and everything seems a bit more forgiving. Our daily mileage has grown, and we frequently complete seventy-mile days. Both of us feel strong. We see motorcyclists on the roads and find that there is an unknown alliance between all people traveling on two wheels. Often, they stop and talk with us, praising our efforts and comparing their challenges to ours. I think of us as the geeks and them as the cool dudes, but out here, it seems like we are comrades. The hills are different out here than on the East Coast. They are big and wide and open. They beckon us to climb higher and higher, promising ever wider vistas. Somehow, they seem gentle.

The climb to Hoosier Pass is a two-day ordeal. The route takes us up from Hot Sulphur Springs, through Silverthorne, and on into Breckenridge. We spend the night here, after a seventy-three-mile uphill day, using it as a sort of base camp for our final ascent.

The culture in Breckenridge is vastly different from what we have encountered in the last few weeks. It is wealthy and privileged. It is a land of lattes and pho noodle soup with linen napkins. Everyone here is healthy and good-looking and seems to divide their days between yoga, outdoor adventure, and shopping. The streets are lined with boutiques and fine dining spots with a backdrop of the Rocky Mountains. A little bit of elite paradise.

Oakley and I stroll the streets in the gathering darkness like children in Disney World. We dine in a Thai restaurant and delight in huge plates full of drunken noodle, piping hot and spicy. Tonight, we will stay in a hostel that has a hot tub and chandeliers made from blue elk antlers. This is living.

As the sun sinks below the mountains, we stop in the shops and fondle polished gems and funny hats. The rings, pendants, and stones glow under the display lights. Oakley and I hold up beautiful specimens and exclaim at their beauty. I wander toward the back of the store to look at the fossils when suddenly I get that tingly feeling. I have let my guard down, and I know better. As I turn about to better keep an eye on Oakley, I am stopped by a salesperson.

"Would you like to see some more fossils?" she asks.

"Um, that's okay. I . . ." My eyes are on Oakley, who is standing behind her back with a Gollum-like look in his eyes and his hands deep in a box of copper rings, letting his fingers dance over all of them.

Oakley, no!

He picks one up and pops it on his finger. He looks up and scans the store. Our eyes meet. In that minute, he knows that I know. He puts the ring back and quickly takes a step back from the display. He flushes.

I quickly hustle us out of the store and into the safety of the night.

"Oakley," I say, "I think you have a problem."

"I know."

"Case of the sticky fingers?"

He looks at me, surprised that I am not freaking out. "I guess."

"What are we going to do? We don't want you ending up like that boy in the striped suit in the basement of the Walden Courthouse."

"I won't!"

"You will. How about we stay out of stores for a while, or you stay by me? Just until you outgrow this temptation. Getting arrested out here would be a pretty big nightmare."

"Okay. I don't mean to do it." He looks at the sidewalk glumly.

"It is going to be okay." And I know it is. I will be on his team until we figure it out.

When we climb into our bunks that night, I am nervous. The idea of Hoosier Pass is unnerving me. There is snow in the forecast, and it could make crossing very unpleasant. I am also aware that I have been afraid of something every day since this trip began—okay, before it began—and I believe I am struggling with fear fatigue. I toss and turn, listening to Oakley's exhausted snores above me. He has been increasingly testy with me, and I have become increasingly short with him. I am sure the constant anxiety we have been feeling isn't helping. Finally, I drift off, aware that fear doesn't stop anything from coming, and I will just have to deal with tomorrow . . . tomorrow.

In the morning, we wake early, suit up, and head out. It is ten miles to the top. It is cold, and the higher we go, the colder it gets. This is actually somewhat motivating, as it encourages us to not stop or we become instantly chilled. Oakley takes the lead and checks behind him at every hairpin bend in the ascent to see if I am still with him.

He looks down at me from above. "Come on, Mom! This is it." I look up at his shining face and try to smile through the agony that is coursing through my thighs. He is definitely stronger than me now, and I appreciate his patience on the steeper sections.

"Yep, I'm a-coming," I wheeze, and on we go. Oakley can truly do absolutely anything if he needs to. I reckon back to all his complaining on our little rides through Portland, our twenty-mile jaunts, and how he now is leading me over the Rockies with a smile. He is in his full glory, and I am glad to be on his team.

"Come on, we are almost there!" he shouts. This is his rite of passage, our rite of passage. I believe that everybody needs these moments when they find their edge, climb their peaks, and sail their seas to find just how strong they are. Not just physically, but emotionally, mentally, and spiritually.

Back and forth we cut, higher and higher. Snow covers the ground all around us, and then there it is: the sign for Hoosier Pass. It stands proudly in a parking lot with several tourists posing for pictures with ear-to-ear smiles. We practically fall off our bikes when we arrive. We are greeted by cheers.

"Did you just bike that?" asks more than one astounded person. Oakley and I beam with pride. We have done it. We are on the top of the world. We have completed half of our mileage and half of our total time on this trip. Our sweat is freezing on our skin—and we can't stop grinning.

"You two are a marvel."

We kind of are. "Geez, thanks," we reply with swelled heads.

Then Oakley, as cool as can be, feels the need to put the icing on the cake.

"Mom," he says, "now I need to do my backflip." Up Oakley climbs, onto the sign, and faces away from the crowd toward the high surrounding peaks. He hesitates with his arms outstretched, staring out into the distance, then catapults himself skyward, bringing his legs up and over his head with a controlled snap and landing firmly on the pavement.

"Now I am ready," he says casually. And off we go, down and away, teeth chattering and toes freezing from this alpine tundra. We can't get down fast enough. We pass buffalo, we pass an elk, we pass a mustang horse. When we reach our campsite after an eighty-eight-mile day, we can barely walk. I limp up to the front counter. "Hi, we need a tent site for the night."

"Are you biking?"

"Yes, we just biked Hoosier Pass. We are beat."

"We don't take bikers."

"What? Why?"

"They always make the biggest problems. They trash the place."

"Bikers? Like pedaling-around bikers?" I ask incredulously.

"Yes. They have ruined it for everyone. There is another campground three miles down the road by the Royal Gorge. They will let you stay, but I will never have another biker sleep here."

Oakley and I are shocked, all our glory sliced through. We look at the parking lot of RVs, at the gravel-coated desert. We hear the hum of the air conditioners and generators. *We make a mess?*

When we do eventually find a place to sleep, it is in the sand beside a horse that murmurs late into the night. Much better than a generator. We sleep without the fly on our tent and watch the moon rise over the Colorado desert as we drift off—a much better sight than a stinking RV.

"Why can't we tour the prison?"

"Because they are using a gas chamber as a playground in the front yard, and I think that is disgusting."

"No, they're not. You are such an exaggerator. It is cool."

"No, I won't glorify such awfulness. Let's go."

"I want to eat lunch at a restaurant."

"No, Oakley, we have food. We need to make tracks."

"Not enough food. We never have enough."

"Yes, we do. Keep pedaling. You are driving me crazy."

"You are driving me crazy!"

And thus begins our morning after the big glorious descent from Hoosier Pass. Oakley is a mess, crabby and tired and full of post-glory letdown. Today was destined to be full of begging, then complaining, and then begging again. I cycle ahead of him and try to gain some distance. "Let's bike in silence."

"No."

Ugh.

And so it goes for the first ten miles of the day, both of us twitchy and stressed as we continue making our way from the Rockies. We bike along a narrow two-lane road that snakes through rock outcroppings and foothills. It is tricky to navigate and heavily trafficked. Oakley is angrily riding right on my tail, refusing to give me my much-needed space.

Suddenly, I hear a truck engine brake behind us. I turn to look over my shoulder and see the front of an enormous truck, adorned with a bright yellow "OVERSIZE LOAD" banner on its grill, twenty feet behind us. There is no room for both an oversize truck and our bikes on this road, bracketed as it is by steep cliffs. I can't immediately swerve off the road and out of the way because there is no shoulder, only sand, and at this speed I would surely wipe out. The only choice is to stop and let the truck have as much of the road as we can give.

"Oakley," I call frantically, "stopping!" That is shorthand for "Heads-up, don't crash into me." But this time Oakley doesn't hear me over the growl of the engine brake. In fact, as I call, he is looking back himself to see what is making the roar behind us. I stop, he doesn't. With his head still turned over his shoulder, he careens into the back of my bike. I feel the crash, and in a horrifying instant, I see him spill out onto the road, his panniers, bike, and body splayed out on the tarmac in front of the oncoming truck. I see his beautiful body, outlined by the yellow oversize banner only a few feet behind. The truck brakes, and the world stops.

A truck coming from the opposite direction stops abruptly as well, and I drop my bike and walk through the stopped traffic to Oakley lying in the road. I help him up. His whole body is trembling.

"It's okay, Oakley." I feel nothing. A numbness has descended over me. "Let's collect your stuff."

As if in a dream, I gather his panniers and bike from the road and look up into the eyes of the trucker. He appears badly shaken and holds his head in his hands. "Thank you," I mouth.

Once Oakley is safely off the road and traffic has commenced, he continues to shake. His kneecaps visibly jump, and the muscles in his arms twitch spasmodically. His fear begins to come out as anger and fury. He screams at me for stopping short. He screams at me for taking him on this reckless adventure. He screams at me and screams at me and screams at me until he stops shaking. But I don't feel a thing. It is like I am watching him from a million miles away, seeing his lips move but hearing nothing. When he recovers, we get on our bikes and continue. What else is there to do?

We battle headwind for the next fifty miles, both of us emotionally spent. When we finally arrive at our designated campsite for the evening, a state park in Pueblo, Colorado, we are relieved to see that it is comprised of a beautifully lush meadow along the banks of the Saint Charles Reservoir. A dip in that cool, clear water will be just the thing to help us regain our composure. I ride up to the entrance gate, incredibly glad to be finished for the day.

"Hello. Boy, are we glad to be here. We have had quite a day. Can we have a tent site for the night?"

"I am sorry, we are full. There is another site ten miles further on." The attendant whips out a map and shows me. It is ten miles in the wrong direction. I think I would be hard-pressed to convince Oakley or myself to sign up for that.

"Oh, that is terrible. We are biking across country and just had a near miss. We really need to stop. We don't even need a site. We can sleep behind the dumpster for all I care. We just can't keep biking."

"I am sorry, but there is a fishing tournament. You won't be able to stay here."

"This is a safety issue. Please."

"Sorry, ma'am, the police will come by and make you leave."

"We are on bikes. They wouldn't really make us, would they?" I gesture at Oakley. "He is a kid!"

"Sorry, but I can't help you."

It is the lowest we have felt. We have been turned away two nights in a row, and Oakley is a wreck because of his accident. But back on our bikes we go, wending our way not to the site ten miles behind but into the city of Pueblo, Colorado, right to the Marriott Hotel. We approach the counter dripping with sweat and fatigue. The room is $170 a night, but luckily for us, a friend has donated a one-night stay at any Marriott on our trip. The sweet woman at the counter sees how much the day has aged me and gives us a senior citizen discount.

We stagger into the elevator, pushing our trusty, worn steeds before us, and smile apologetically at the other guests that enter our odor circle. The room's clean white sheets, soft white pillows, air conditioning, and hot showers provide an unprecedented luxury. After cleaning the day's horror and grit from my body, I sit in a fluffy white towel on the side of the bed and call Twain.

I tell him about what our day has entailed. How scary it was. What a close call it was.

He is far more shaken than I anticipated. "You can come home, you know . . . you don't have to do this. You crossed Hoosier Pass . . . you guys have done enough. You have nothing to prove."

I am shocked. Quitting hasn't occurred to me, and I realize that Twain has no idea how scary this has been every day in so many different ways, but also how worth it this has been. The fear is part of the beauty, the aliveness. However, I consider that maybe I have lost my ability to think clearly about acceptable risk and decide that at least I should consult Oakley. After all, it is his life that was compromised. When I get off the phone, I sit Oakley down beside me.

"Papa mentioned that we could quit if we wanted. We could, you know. If you really wanted to. We have crossed the Rockies; that is pretty cool." Oakley's forehead wrinkles, and he looks at me like I am out of my mind.

"We aren't quitting!" he responds. "Papa's crazy! He doesn't get it. We have to finish." Quitting had never occurred to him either. It is at this moment that we both realize that we are going to make it. Then we go out to dinner and eat until all we can do is waddle our way back to our beds.

Oakley's Two Cents

Highs and Lows

Okay, so my mom probably has told you guys about this, but on Friday the 13th I believe I almost died. We were biking down a fairly busy road when an overloaded truck came up behind us. My mom saw the big truck and called to me, "Stopping!" so we could get out of the way, but she was not loud enough for me to hear. I had turned my head to look at what was hulking behind me. When I turned my head back around, I crashed into my mom's slowing bike and tumbled right in front of that giant overloaded truck. THAT, my friend, was the scariest moment in my LIFE.

Anyway, now for the high. My high is getting out of the Rockies. We did our last huge pass a couple days ago right outside Breckenridge, Colorado. The pass was really hard, but it was worth it.

We are halfway done with this trip. In no time we will be across Kansas, and then into Missouri and Kentucky, which I'm not excited about at all. Kentucky dogs, here I come. I feel really happy that we have gotten this far, and I know that there is no turning back now that we have made such good progress.

I Fall Apart

September 17–26, 2019

Kansas

After Colorado, it will be flat! Pretty much all downhill to the East Coast. The winds in our country are generally eastbound, so the wind will be at our backs the rest of the way. We can sail! With this hope and expectation in our hearts, we sally forth toward Kansas full of good cheer and vibrato. We have crossed the Rockies and cycled over the Continental Divide eight times. What can possibly stop us now?

The wind. God help us, the wind. Let me just say that the winds found on the Colorado and Great Plains are a force as strong as the tide and as big as the sky. They blow at a sustained thirty-plus knots with gusts up to sixty. All the time. We are drowning in it.

It is hard to catch our breath as we slog across the plains. Dirt and dust blow up from the overcultivated fields and feedlots, and a haze of yellow grit has formed over the land, reducing visibility like a dense buttery fog. This grit burns our eyes, gets in our ears, parches our throats, and covers our skin with a coat of grime. I have a sneaking suspicion that it is heavily laden with pesticides.

At night our tent shudders and flaps in the wind and does not lend itself to a solid night's sleep. We have been sleeping in city parks every night, in towns that feel ghostly because everyone else is hiding inside.

Oakley looks like he has a drug problem. His eyes have become squinty and red, and he refuses to wear his sunglasses. His bottom lip is split and swollen, and he refuses to wear sunscreen on it. Why, you might ask? Because I ask him to. This brings me to my second vexation about the wind: It gets inside you. It tunnels into your ears and up your nose and wreaks havoc on your brain—and your spirit.

Every day the wind blows, Oakley and I get on each other's nerves a little more. I am annoying. I speak annoyingly, chew annoyingly, and, according to Oakley, I have suddenly become deaf. Oakley is also annoying. He talks too much, steps on the tent, and has bad manners. He is 100 percent sixteen years old, which is annoying in itself. I know this is just the wind working its wicked ways, and, luckily, Oakley knows it too.

In many ways this is a more difficult challenge than the passes we have ascended. This is grueling, solitary, and boring. It lacks glory. But when I look up and see Oakley, slowly but methodically plugging along through the wind and heat, alone in his thoughts hour after hour because the wind makes it too hard to talk, I am sure there is good in this stage. This too is important.

We have taken to retreating into town libraries every afternoon and reading for hours. We fantasize about iced tea constantly. We seek out mom-and-pop movie theaters. We go for walks when the evenings cool. And at least once a day we forgive each other for our snappy behavior and acknowledge that we are in this together.

The wind is supposed to quiet tomorrow, and I am hoping to be able to look out upon these beautiful plains without squinting, to absorb the incredibly wide expanse of land that is far larger and flatter than I have ever comprehended.

Yesterday, a local woman blew into the library, and I overheard her say, "If there is one woman in Kansas who doesn't use hairspray, I don't know her! It is the only way to survive!" Maybe if the wind doesn't die down, we will try that next. It can't hurt.

Eastern Colorado and Kansas are full of soy, milo, corn, feedlots, and silos. As we cycle across the plains, we often set our sights on an enormous silo looming up out of the clouds of dust from over fifteen miles away. We set our course for these mirage-like behemoths and pedal toward them as if they are lighthouses at sea. Time and again we fantasize about the cute little cafés with cool drinks within that are sure to be nestled in their shade. They never are.

More often, we find scenes from *Star Wars*, where one can imagine Jawas striding through the yellow clouds of dust to get back to their sand crawlers that blink in and out of sight through the haze, without a human in sight. Chaff blows up against the walls of the silos, and grain husks pile up around their bases. Some days there is so much particulate matter in the air that we are advised not to bike for health reasons. We do bike though, every day, because we are headed for a treat. Twain will be flying into Wichita, Kansas, and joining us for a week. In order to meet him on the appointed day, we have to average sixty-five miles a day. In wind like we are experiencing, this is proving quite a task.

Every day, as soon as the sky grows light, we crawl from our tents. We quickly pack up our gear and try to get as far as we can before the wind kicks in. Usually that is around 10:00 in the morning. Then we slog through it until around 2:00 in the afternoon, when we fall into the arms of a small town, seeking relief and shelter from the relentless howling.

The towns that are sprinkled through rural Kansas seem to be clinging to life by a wisp. Most of the storefronts are empty, the wide streets ghostly. You can tell that in the farming heyday they were prosperous and full of the bustle of country folk, but now many are completely abandoned, and those that are left seem doomed. Big agriculture has come in with its big monocrops and machines and chemicals. They've stripped the land and pillaged the towns. It is rather disheartening.

There are a large number of huge penitentiaries that have sprung up in this area. Human incarceration seems to have replaced the family farm as an industry. It does nothing to improve the desolate feeling of some of these towns, but it does populate them in several ways. The prisons create jobs for people and draw the families of food service workers, guards, maintenance workers, and mechanics to a few of these otherwise doomed towns. The prisoners themselves also populate the area. When they are released, they often decide to settle locally. Many of them are challenged with poverty or obtaining employment, and these small rural towns seem to struggle to meet their needs.

Here in western Kansas, I feel a bit ill at ease sleeping alone. One town sounds a siren at 8:00 p.m. signaling that everyone has to be in their homes. Not the greatest feeling when you are sleeping in a tent in the city park. Once again, I am glad to have our bear spray.

Oakley is always oblivious to these threats. He has the gift of taking everyone that he meets at face value and accepts people's differences as assets. He is able to make friends in every town we travel to by sidling up to some boys in the park and doing a backflip. Literally, it is his signature move for sparking up conversations. Then he and his newfound crew run about doing parkour and flexing and telling nasty jokes. I just pretend not to notice because these hot and fast friendships allow me a reprieve to call my husband, read, and take a break from being the cruise director of our voyage. When I mention occasionally that I don't think it feels very safe in certain towns, he scolds me: "Mom, you are so uptight!"

I remind him that I am sleeping in city parks, eating gas station food, biking along highways, and peeing behind guardrails—so "uptight" might not be an accurate descriptor. This falls on deaf ears.

There is another, more joyful side of life in these towns too. They aren't all despair and heartache. The people who live here seem to live in another era—one in which the grocery store is closed on Sundays. The town theater is only open on Saturday and Sunday nights for a family movie at five, to which half the town comes. Ice cream cones cost $1.25. Farmers still show up at the hardware store in their overalls to discuss the weather. The county fair is a really big deal, with the biggest sky in the world as a backdrop.

In each of these towns we seek a library to retreat to and spend our afternoons hiding from the sun and the wind and working on homeschooling. Oakley is required to read, journal, do half an hour of math, and create a weekly blog. These tasks, though annoying, often give shape to our afternoons. When evening comes, we find the local city park and set up our tent under the playground, hoping to avoid the sprinklers that are sure to turn on at 2:00 a.m. We read aloud until our eyes droop, oblivious to the glare of the streetlights, and then we pass out to the noise of the tent's fly flapping.

Oakley and I decide that if we are ever going to do a century ride, Kansas is the place. We wait for a windless day, which thankfully does eventually come, and go for it—100 miles in a day. Our spirits are high, and we sail through fields of milo and corn. We make fifty-five miles before lunch and flex our huge thigh muscles at each other, posturing like the Hulk. Tonight, we will sleep in a fair-sized town, so we will go out to dinner, restock our supplies, and live it up. This allows us to pack lightly on food and to have something to look forward to as a reward for our efforts.

We saddle up again and head off. The miles drop off behind us, and the fields give way to trees. Trees! Little forests. We are overjoyed. We are getting somewhere. Then, at eighty-three miles, pop! Of course.

Oakley screams from behind me, "Mom, stop!"

I cringe. Another flat. What a waste of time.

When I circle back to help him and offer moral support, I quickly see that it is worse than I imagined. The pop was not a flat tire; it was his spokes starting to go—two of them. The wheel has the telltale wobble, and try as I might, I can't get it true despite how many pencils I lash in place with duct tape. We are stranded. It is late. Up ahead I see a sign for a public restroom, and we trudge along the roadway toward it. Maybe there will be someone there to give us a ride?

When we arrive, we find that it is the tidiest restroom we have ever come across. The walls, floors, sinks, and toilets sparkle. There is a men's and a women's side, and a tiny vestibule. That's it. It is heavily air-conditioned, and we stand in that vestibule a long time trying to figure out what to do. There are no cars on this road, just large transport trucks, some carrying loads as big as silos and underground gas tanks. I have never seen such loads, and we have been flagged off the road by many support vehicles throughout the day. I try to hitchhike, but only half-heartedly. These trucks are not picking us up. The sun is setting. Here we will stay.

We set up our tent under a glaring parking lot light and eat a supper of instant noodles mixed with canned tuna. We are still hungry. Oakley is restless. Periodically, a huge truck pulls into the lot, and Oakley visits with the drivers. Some of them take the time to show him their engines, some crawl into their sleeper cabs to take a wee nap, and some set about washing their rigs. The evening wears on. When we crawl into our very hot tent, I am suddenly aware of how visible we are. There is nobody around but random truckers, and once again I sleep with my bear spray in my hands. It is turning into the best fifty dollars that I ever spent.

The next day we are fortunate enough to hitch a ride with a man and his son. They drive us forty miles out of their way (and ours) to a bike shop. For all my fear of scary strangers, I am meeting only kindness. Oakley is proven right again and again: people are good, and I am uptight.

The next day, I buy him a Bluetooth speaker and let him blast music for fifty miles all the way to Newton, Kansas, where we will meet my husband. We cycle through the last tall prairie grass refuge in the United States, listening to Queen. "We Are the Champions" seems fitting.

The night before my husband joins us for a week of riding is like Christmas Eve. As I lay in my bed at the Comfort Inn in Newport, Kansas, waiting for him to arrive on a 10:30 p.m. flight, I am overwhelmed with excitement.

Finally, after seven weeks, I am going to have an adult partner to share all my responsibilities, decisions, and parenting with. What fun we will have! How much I have missed him! Oakley and I have rushed to get here, pushing ourselves over the Rockies at a breakneck pace, three weeks of sixty-plus-mile days—and we have made it. All there is to do is lie in this cozy bed and wait. I hope he will wake me with a kiss.

So I wait. Happy and content and . . . chilled? I begin to toss and turn. Maybe it is the air-conditioning. Maybe I am just excited. I burrow deeper into the covers.

Finally, Twain arrives. But as he climbs into bed and cozies up beside me, rather than feeling elated, I feel sure that something is amiss.

It must have come from a combination of breathing in windblown feedlot nasties, wearing sweat-sodden clothes for weeks at a time, and exhaustion. As he gleefully announces that he is here and does indeed give me a much-awaited kiss, I murmur, "I think we have one small problem," and feel my fever skyrocket.

Thus begins our week together. I diagnose myself with a terrible case of non-lactating mastitis. My breast turns scarlet red and grows cement hard. It swells into my armpit. Even on antibiotics, my fever rages for six days. As strong as I have been, I am that weak. Twain cooks, sets up the tent, banters with Oakley, and cleans the dishes while I sit watching through rheumy eyes like a hopped-up queen. All I am in charge of is pedaling.

One night, we come to a small town called Cassoday. It is nearly impossible to tell what the residents might do for a living. There is no industry here that we can see. We are directed to the city park, which is not much more than a grassy patch with train tracks running along-side. Oakley sets up the tent, and Twain whips up a pot of beans and rice. A freight train sails by, blaring its horn just in case one of the town people are picnicking on the tracks, I suppose. This park has no toilets, so we take turns relieving ourselves in the shrubbery along the tracks. Another train hurries by, sounding its alarming horn. We scurry back to the grass. Then another train. And another. They will come every thirty minutes, blasting their horns and jarring us again and again all night long.

My fever is raging. I crawl into the tent and shake. This park has no sink, just a pump that spews oily water that tastes tainted by fracking. A neighbor works hopefully on creating a RV park in her backyard, for what potential travelers, I know not. Twain does his best to stay upbeat. He laughs at the craziness and tussles with Oakley. I think I fall apart because, for the first time, I can.

A Tent Kitten

September 26–October 5, 2019

Missouri

Kansas slowly turns into Missouri, and the landscape begins to cooperate with my illness. All that fierce, hot, dry wind that has been plaguing us abates. The land becomes soft and green, filled with cows, turtles, frogs, and beautiful horses. The small towns that we travel through provide homemade pie, even for breakfast. Twain only feels up to biking fifty miles a day. We pass snakes, armadillos, and a badger. The earth has become welcoming again. Perfect.

Oakley and I enjoy watching Twain adjust to our standards of living because, truth be told, they are low. He gags on our peanut butter tacos. Struggles with insomnia in our hot, fetid tent, sleeping with his shorts half on and half off, too hot to bear the waistband gripping his sweaty belly and too shy to go without in case he needs to launch suddenly from the tent into the public parks we sleep in. He's disgusted by using public bathrooms that are literally smeared with feces. And he struggles when we bike up the first punishing hills of the Ozarks as the humidity renders all of our muscles soggy.

Still, he is a champ and maintains his good humor, lavishing praise and affection on us. In fact, I think it helps Oakley's and my morale to see how hard this is for a newbie.

This morning as Twain and I bike away from each other at the Fall Festival in Fair Grove, Missouri, he to the airport and Oakley and I into the heart of the Ozarks, tears are squirting out of my eyes. It's not that I don't want to be doing this; it's that I have had a taste of comfort and care, and it makes me wickedly homesick. It is when you taste softness that you realize what hardness is.

Rain is falling hard as we head out of town. I feel depleted. I am physically strong again, but my heart is heavy. *Gosh, this is a long trip,* I think. Oakley is acting cowed by my outpouring of emotion. I am supposed to be the strong one, and here I am, a blubbering mess. I notice that Oakley is giving me a break from his complaining and his chatter.

"We only have less than a month left, Mom. We are going to be fine."

"I know," I snivel.

After a day of wet riding, we arrive in Hartville, Missouri. The sun breaks through the clouds and turns the wet pavement into a hot steam bath. "Okay, let's get some treats to buoy our spirits." Oakley, not one to ever turn down sweets, or any snack for that matter, happily agrees that a snack is just the thing to help me get my game on.

We stop in a gas station and ask for directions to the grocery store that is labeled on our map. Even in a small town, it seems somehow to be hiding from view.

"The grocery store is gone," says the cashier. "It blew away in a tornado just two weeks ago. You need to go over to Fair Grove for food. It is only about forty-five minutes that way." He gestures toward the town from which we have just come.

"You're kidding me."

"No, it was blown away. You should go look. It's pretty cool." Oakley is eager to go check out the destruction, so we do. The building has been obliterated. A wide swath of destruction cuts through the middle, revealing metal beams jackknifing towards the sky, a sea of overturned shelves, and rotten food.

We head to our designated camping spot in the town park about a half mile outside town. It is beautifully set on the grassy banks of a sluggish river full of turtles and fish. However, the algae are in full bloom, as are the mosquitos, and there is no potable water. We retreat back to town and find some semi-poisonous food in the form of a gas station pizza. I am sweaty and emotional and decide we should call it a night even though the sun has not yet set.

I climb into our tent to seek refuge from all the bugs. Miraculously, Oakley continues with his good humor, filling in where I have none. Perhaps he is emulating his father.

"I will be in soon," he says. "I am just going to explore a little."

In a few minutes I hear him calling, "Mom! Mom! I have a surprise!" He unzips the door and thrusts in a small kitten like it is the greatest gift I could ever hope for. He jumps in behind it, grinning from ear to ear.

"It's a stray!" he asserts.

The cat wanders all around, brushing its fur up against our sweaty skin, leaving tufts of hair everywhere and threatening to pop our air mattresses.

"Tonight we will have a tent kitten! Isn't that cozy?"

Is he crazy? A tent kitten? I begin to object, but then I look at the delight shining in Oakley's eyes.

"Toughen up, Mom. Home will be there! Look how cute he is!"

In this moment I am wildly thankful for my traveling partner. I am often quick to brag about his physical gifts and at the same time disparage his behavior, but at this moment, listening to him trying to cheer me up, I can wholeheartedly say that I think he is amazing. It is not lost on me that what he is accomplishing is nothing short of incredible.

For fifty-eight days now, he has woken up beside his mother (hard enough in itself), packed up our tent on his own, and then hit the road for six to eight hours of cycling. He averages sixty miles a day and carries more weight than his dear old ma. He has climbed all the hills, eaten all the nasty food, traversed all the windy deserts, slept on all the concrete and sodden ground, all without bailing out on me or outright refusing to go further, and right now he is trying to be nice.

He has told me endless stories (specifically, every single superhero movie in detail) to entertain us both. He has encouraged me again and again when I despaired after losing our way. Most people would have brained me!

Yes, sometimes, he loses his good humor and lapses into blaming me for all wrongs, but it is always short-lived. He even apologizes. Yes, he has a problem with sticky fingers and impulse control, but he is dealing with this head-on, admitting it, and trying to make changes. And at the end of every long day, he has been doing schoolwork—math, writing, and reading—and then putting up our tent. That is a tremendous gift, trust me.

It is a great challenge to spend this much time with any one person, and I don't deny that he does drives me crazy. I know that I drive him crazy, too, but in this moment of clarity, I just can't believe that he is doing this—that we seem to have found a way to fill in each other's weakness with strength.

Home feels like a mythical place at this point, but I am going to follow Oakley's lead and rediscover my strength. Home will be waiting. I decide to let the cat stay for an hour or two and read out loud to Oakley while he gives it cuddles. Its contented purring fills the tent.

In the morning, as we are packing up our bikes, a man with long gray hair leans out of his old Chevy pickup truck and calls out a warning: "There are hills coming up, and some of them are going to be severe!"

Nobody. Ever. Told. Me. About. The. Ozarks. Who knew that these mountains—which don't even show up on most maps of the United States—could be more physically punishing than the Rocky Mountains? Up and down and up and down, like a heart monitor. The full-body exertion required to climb these acute hills feels similar to childbirth. While climbing them, I lapse into Lamaze breathing several times. The sweat pours down my cheeks and hangs beard-like off my chin. I beg the heavens above for ice chips. I become nonverbal. I do think the Ozarks are incredibly beautiful, but I never need to do this again.

By night we sleep in American Legions, Lions Clubs, and inexpensive or free hostels. We microwave our dinners and try desperately to get cool. The people open up their towns to us, and Oakley feels welcomed everywhere we go, but there are no other bikers. The last one we saw was weeks ago. We have met a total of only twelve on this trip.

One was a veteran that was on a six-month roundabout trip, spreading the respect for people of all professions that risk their lives, from vets to police officers to firefighters. We camped with him and exchanged stories around a campfire late into the night. He ended his trip biking through Los Angeles escorted by fire trucks.

There was Shane, an ER nurse who had left his wife at home for a month tour, and although he was having fun, he felt heartbroken with missing her. We camped with him for a few nights and encouraged each other.

There was Joe, a firefighter himself, who was doing 100 to 120 miles a day solo, in straight head-to-toe flaming spandex. Literally, the spandex was covered in a flame pattern. He put us to shame.

There were the two brothers from Germany, both in their sixties. They had started in Yorktown, Virginia, together, and by the time they made it to Montana, they'd decided to finish separately. "Too much togetherness," they said.

There was Brian and Kate, traveling as boyfriend and girlfriend. What a test of a new relationship. They had two months to complete the course from start to finish. But we saw those people all months ago now. There has been nobody for weeks.

We were told at the TransAmerica headquarters that over one thousand complete the trail every year. Where are they? Are we too late? I feel the stress of needing to cross the Appalachians before it gets much cooler. Maybe all the other bikers know something that we do not.

The Mississippi River. Never have Oakley and I been so happy to see a river in our lives. As our bikes touch down on the alluvial soil of the Missouri side, a weight feels lifted from my shoulders. Surely the hardest struggles are behind us. In three weeks, we will be home. The land opening up before us is covered with prosperous farms and vibrant crops. We turn toward the river, getting ready to cross the bridge that will spill us into the East, when we encounter a heavily loaded recumbent cyclist coming towards us. The thirteenth biker! We hurriedly cross the road to chat.

The man seems equally eager to connect with a fellow cyclist, and he comes quickly to a stop. He is probably in his late fifties and sports a long gray beard. His hair hangs limply in long greasy tendrils from under his helmet. His skin is leathery and worn, and his body is emaciated, all skin and bones. Behind his recumbent bike he pulls a plywood trailer the size of a large coffin.

"Hi there! Where are you coming from?" we ask.

The man untangles himself from his unit. When he stands he seems stork-like. "Everywhere. I have been riding for nineteen years."

"Nineteen years?!" Oakley and I gape at each other. Perhaps he is the ghost of things to come.

"Yeah, I love it. Started and never stopped. Let me show you my rig." We wander over to his trailer, and he opens a little door on the side of the plywood wall. "I built this myself. It is nine hundred pounds." On the inside of the door, he has written all the states that he has cycled through, some several times. "I have my bed in here, and my stove, supplies, solar power batteries, and a television."

"Wow, that is incredible."

"It is heavy. Sometimes I only make twenty miles a day. I take freeways when I can because they are less hilly than back roads."

Is this man crazy? A modern nomad? Homeless? He continues to talk, and Oakley and I continue to listen, but after some time, I get the feeling that we may be there until sunset. This man is one lonely biker, and we have miles to go.

"Okay, well, we have to head off," I interrupt. "We have far to go to get to our campsite tonight."

Now the man looks at me blankly.

"If you have a rig like this, you don't need a campsite. You just pull over. No worries."

Oakley and I climb astride our bikes and push off. Our hundred-pound loads feel far lighter, the distance we have to go far shorter, and the length of time until we will be home briefer than ever before.

"Mom, he was so cool!"

I stare at Oakley incredulously. "Cool? I think he was crazy!"

"You are so uptight!" And off we go to the Mississippi.

Oakley's Two Cents

My Dad Can't Hack It

This week my dad flew into Wichita, Kansas, and got a ride to Newton, where we are, to bike with us for the week. While we were biking, my mother and I were annoyed to see my dad biking very fast on his not-so-heavily-weighted bike. He barely carried anything, and he kept acting like it was easy! He also only liked to go forty to fifty miles a day. So it was an easy week for me too.

A couple of days after he had joined us, we were biking along, and I (of course) crashed again from hitting the back of my mother's bike while trying to point out a big frog on the side of the road. I ended up sprawled across the ground, and my bike wound up in a ditch in the bushes on the other side of the road.

While I collected myself, my dad offered to get my bike out the bushes and trade bikes with me for the last seven miles of the ride. He could barely pull my bike out of the ditch! He complained that it weighed as much as a tank. "Tank" is my bike's new name.

Now we have reached the Ozark Mountains and have quickly realized that as soon as my dad leaves, my mom and I are going to hit the worst of them. He is so lucky.

The Ozarks are rolling hills that are absolutely straight up and down with no switchbacks again and again. They are the worst. Hopefully, we will be out of them in four days.

We only have about four weeks left and then we are done. I can't believe our progress, and I thank my mom for all the great adventures we have been through and for the adventures ahead.

The Great Mississippi

October 6-10, 2019

Illinois

We cross the wide, lazy Mississippi River unceremoniously, on a narrow bridge with cars and trucks honking at us to get out of the way. We want to stop and take in its majesty, but we are hurried along. If you can't slow down and feel lazy along this river, where can you?

The land has flattened out. The river's floodplain stretches out for miles on either side and has created a fertile flat farming paradise, blanketed by rich soil carried down from upstream over eons. It beckons us to come coast and relax along the wide, muddy river.

We spend a night in Chester, Illinois, the home of Popeye the Sailor Man. There are statues of him and his compatriots all throughout the town. It is not difficult to imagine them swashbuckling on and off barges and around the docks. This is a working town, full of people whose livelihood is still built upon the river and surrounding land. We are told that tourists only come here once a year for the annual Popeye Picnic festival. It is world-renowned.

In the morning, we ride up levees and look down on miles of farm fields and flooded forests filled with frogs. The air is humid and thick even early in the morning. We watch idly as quarter-mile-long barges slowly maneuver up and down the river. The pull to continue south with the Mississippi proves too much. It puts us into a contented, self-satisfied stupor. We ride for hours with a glorious tailwind, watching the water race toward the gulf as we race beside it. Life is good—too good.

I hear my phone ring in my bicycle bag, and I pull over to check who might be calling. It is Twain. "You are going the wrong way!" he shouts into the phone.

"What are you talking about? We are doing great."

"You overshot your turn! I just looked at your location on my phone, and I can see you. You are way past where you need to be."

I stop and check our maps and find that we have missed our turn to the east by fifteen miles—the marvels of modern technology. If Twain hadn't checked where we were, we might have ended up in Louisiana! I try not to tell Oakley, instead turning around and heading back the way we came, right into a headwind. He catches on pretty quick though. The ride back up the river is not nearly as much fun.

Oakley and I are finishing up a seventy-four-mile day. Evening is coming, and we find ourselves on a back road on the Illinois/Kentucky border (the Illinois side of the Ohio River) with no idea where to go. The campsite that was supposed to be here isn't. We are exhausted and growing irritable. In desperation, I begin searching for a house in the hopes of asking someone if we can stay in their backyard. Oakley is none too chuffed about this idea. I think he is imagining a scene from *Psycho.*

From up ahead I sense activity and decide to push on just a wee bit more. Oakley groans. As we round the corner, we are rewarded in spades for our perseverance. There before us lies the small town of Rosiclare, population 350, the entirety of which are out in the street celebrating the Fluorspar Festival. You might ask, What is fluorspar? I soon discover that it is a mineral found in many important things, including fluoride; that it's the state mineral of Illinois; and that the town was founded on the discovery of fluorspar beneath its soil many years ago. Rosiclare was once referred to as the Fluorspar Capital of the World.

There, by the side of the Ohio River, we soon forget our aches and pains as we eat fried food, lemon shake-ups, and funnel cake. We watch the town's bike parade, pet parade, golf cart parade, and street dance party, complete with red, blue, and green spinning disco lights. The party goes late into the night, way past our bedtime. Yay for fluorspar! It is now our favorite element.

Late that night, Oakley and I crawl into our tent and nestle into our sleeping bags in the Rosiclare city park by the side of the Ohio River in the midst of all other fluorspar revelers. The wide Ohio runs serenely beside us, and we can hear it lapping on its banks. We both feel tired and contented. Satiated. This is what our trip is all about. The gift of safety after danger, ease after hardship, and strength after weakness. Who knows what will happen tomorrow? Tonight feels perfect.

Oakley's Two Cents
Surprises in the Middle of Nowhere

Once we passed through the Ozarks, we crossed the Mississippi and came into this town called Chester, Illinois. It happens to be where Popeye was "born." The original creator was born there, and the comic is based on the area and the local people. The town was filled of statues of all the characters.

That night we stayed in this shack which was supposed to be the bike hostel. We were grateful for the place to stay and the showers, but the spot was more like a little closet. We didn't know that we were passing through Illinois until we actually got there. Other than the shack, Illinois was really beautiful. We biked through lush tree-filled forests, and there were little hills that were not too steep.

A couple of days ago, we got mixed up and kind of lost. We could not figure out where our campground was, so we asked someone for directions, and they sent us down this back road that went on forever. They had told us that it was "less than a mile down that road." Five miles later we finally came across a little town which had a festival going on that night. We parked our bikes by the Ohio River and went out to the festival and ended up having a great time. We ate a dinner of all fried food.

The next day we crossed the Ohio River into Kentucky. At first, I was dreading the sheer fact of even biking through there because, you know . . . the DOG thing. But I didn't realize Kentucky could be so beautiful. That night we ended up staying in this nice church hostel. The people were really friendly, and they had pool tables, air hockey, and ping-pong tables, plus showers, laundry, and a kitchen. We found out the dreadful dogs are "friendly," and if you just stop your bike, they will realize that you are a human, not something to chase.

Killers and Kittens and Dogs, Oh My!

October 11-19, 2019

Kentucky

"I want to get a bayonet. I am not going into Kentucky without one."

"No."

"Then I want a baseball bat."

"No."

"Then a taser."

"No."

We enter Kentucky with more than a little trepidation. All along our route, we have been warned of dogs—dogs that roam the hills and hollows of Kentucky in wild packs, attacking cyclists. We heard of torn pants, bloodied calves, and ripped-open forearms.

"It is no joke," we have been warned.

"Keep your bear spray at the ready, maybe an air horn."

"Bring a tennis racket and swat them in the nose."

"If you see them, get off your bike and use it as a shield."

"Be careful of trying to outrun them, especially on a hill, because they will get right in front of your tire, and you will crash, and then they will attack you."

It has been hard to calm Oakley down, and it doesn't help that we have had one incident in Montana already. We were cruising down from Lolo Pass toward Missoula, luxuriating in the speed after a long and arduous climb. Suddenly, from out of the bushes barreled a lion-like German Shepherd. He bounded into the roadway, weaving through the traffic, his sights set on us. We could hear his owner shouting in a frenzied pitch, "Duke! Duke! Come! Duke!" Duke didn't care. He didn't even care about the cars and trucks in the roadway, darting between speeding bumpers to get to us. He had only one thing on his mind: our flesh.

"Oakley! Bike!"

"I am!"

Our feet whirled like pinwheels in a fresh breeze, trying to gain purchase on our already downhill speed. I could feel the dog on my heels, and when I turned to see how close he was, I saw bloodthirsty eyes, a wild mane, and teeth lunging toward my ankles.

"Mom, go!" screamed Oakley. We put every ounce of our strength into outdistancing the dog, so much so that we never looked back again because of the millisecond it might slow us down.

Luckily, we made it to safety that time. But now there was Kentucky. *Packs* of dogs?

By the time we ferry across the Ohio River and land in Sebree, Kentucky, Oakley is beside himself. He looks at the shore as we approach, searching for monster dogs in the bushes, or a crazy wanderer, something akin to Deliverance, but the first few days are uneventful. There are dogs, and they do occasionally run out from their farmhouses and yap at our heels, but we end up being more worried about them getting hit by a car than for ourselves.

We spend the night in the basement of a Baptist church in Sebree. Staying there feels bit like entering the land of the lotus-eaters. The church has kitted out its basement with pool tables, a television, foosball, laundry, showers, a kitchen, and comfy couches. One could hide from scary things that go bump in the night, or an attack from the bushes, for a very long time. The price of our accommodations is a conversation with a well-meaning but long-talking minister. Oakley and I sit with him for over an hour as he recounts his long and tiring path to Jesus. We feel a little like hostages. We do our best to remain attentive and polite, but all we want is sleep.

"Well," I say, trying to wrap up the conversation, "we have to get some rest. Thank you so much."

"Okay," said the minister. "If I don't see you in the morning, may Christ go with you. All the bikers coming here from the East tell stories of vicious dogs. They aren't too bad in this area, but east of Berea, they are something. It is a different world."

I think Oakley would have committed his life to Jesus right there if it meant we could stay in this safe, cozy church basement.

We cycle on through beautiful horse country, rolling hills, and stately trees. The people are kind here. They open up firehouses, gazebos, and churches for free to cyclists passing through. It confuses Oakley that the houses and garages frequently fly confederate flags and have Trump signs in their yards and on their bumpers. He points out nearly every one and is jittery whenever we are in a neighborhood with several Confederate flags flanking the road.

"Mom, these people are nice. How can they be so nice to us and still like Trump and fly the Confederate flag? Does that mean that they like slavery?"

This prompts a long political discussion about the many interpretations of the Civil War and the various reasons why someone might support Donald Trump, whom Oakley sees as a maniacal tyrant.

"People can have radically different beliefs and still be kind. I imagine that a lot of people here in rural America feel disrespected and forgotten by our country. They have been struggling, and so they are either looking for something new in Trump or looking at the past through rose-colored glasses, imagining that it was better. They are good people. It is just a different world."

"Yeah, but what if we were Black? Would they be nice then?"

"I am not sure." I think hard about what it would be like to bike across the country as a Black woman with her Black teenage son. It's unsettling to admit that our whiteness makes me feel safer. It feels wrong.

When we reach the town of Berea, we take a much-needed day off. It is an island of privilege and sophistication. Berea College is a liberal-arts school that primarily serves the families of rural Kentucky. Through generous scholarships (due to an enormous endowment and a vibrant work-study program), most of the students attend for free. Free! The school owns the town and lavishes it in citywide activities, opportunities, and programs for all ages. The campus and surrounding area are beautiful. We drink lattes and eat burritos and ice cream while we chat up the locals. Everyone seems so levelheaded.

"What are all these silly tales about dogs?" we ask a professor from the college as we share a coffee table at a lovely café, sure that he will ease our fears.

"Oh, you are heading east? It is a different world out there. They are good people, just different. After you leave here, you are going to ascend a big hill named, aptly, Big Hill. Once you cross over, everything changes. The houses are pressed up against the road because of the narrow hollows. Dogs will pop out at you from everywhere, with no warning. They don't really take kindly to strangers. There are also people known as wanderers. There is a big drug issue, meth mostly. You will be fine, though."

This is not what we want to hear. I was hoping for a pep talk for Oakley . . . and for me.

I try to console Oakley myself. "We have made it this far. We will be fine."

He is not so sure. Of all our challenges, dogs are the most frightening to him.

Tonight, as we get ready to bed down outside the town's fire station, one of the firefighters comes out to check in with us, his kind smile belying his frightening words. "Hey guys, just so you are aware, there is a murderer at large on the other side of Big Hill. Seems a man was released from prison and immediately shot his girlfriend and kidnapped someone. The police can't find him. There is a manhunt underway. You be careful out there."

Oakley is now completely panic-stricken. My stomach wobbles, but I try to put on a brave face. After all, there is only one way home.

"Oakley, nobody is going to kill two bicyclists!" I try to say with assurance. I smile at our informant and try to mime my need for his support.

"I don't know what to tell you," he says.

The next morning, as Oakley loads up his gear, I stop in the fire station to get an update while I am out of his earshot. "Did they catch him?"

"No," reports the firefighter. "In fact, they cancelled school in the next two counties. There are a lot of people looking for him, but there are a lot of places to hide."

"They cancelled school? Because they don't think the children are safe?"

"That is about right."

I try several times to call Twain. I need to hear him tell me that we would be okay if we went on. But he doesn't pick up. It is all on me. When I rejoin Oakley, I am in a stink of fear, and although I speak positively, he is on to me.

"Okay, Oakley, let's do this."

"You're afraid."

"We will be fine."

"You don't know that."

He is absolutely right, but what choice do we have?

As we head out of Berea and up Big Hill, both of us are taut with worry. We begin taking turns telling each other why we are going to be okay. Oakley has his bear spray and an air horn within arm's reach. I attach a stick to my panniers.

It is indeed a different world over Big Hill. There are houses nestled in hollows close to the road with steep hills rising behind them. There is extreme poverty evidenced by decrepit houses, stranded cars, and piles of trash. There are dogs, endless dogs. But every time we see one, we stop, and the dogs stop too. They yap at our heels, but when the chase is over, so is their game, and they wander away.

We do come upon a whole pack of dogs, seven or eight of them, and they bark in a cacophony. We have to walk so they won't chase us, and we end up walking three miles in this dog parade, unable to saddle up and ride on until they have played themselves out. What a sight we are, leading that parade. I use my stick as a baton.

As we cruise up and down the hills, climbing in and out of hollows, we come upon a man standing in the middle of the road. He has long greasy hair and a potbelly that stretches out his too-small, stained gray T-shirt. We stop to ask if he is alright.

"I was driving here, and a black goat just appeared in the road. Made me crash my car." He gestures toward a ditch that we hadn't noticed, and there is a white sedan slumped on its side.

"I am going to need to call my brother. He has a winch, I think."

We see no black goat. Was there a black goat?

Oakley and I do feel like we are in a foreign country, one that perhaps has been forgotten by America. We pass small homes and trailers pressed up against the road with windows made of plastic, roofs repaired with screwed-in plywood, and yards mounded with broken toys, auto parts, and stoves. One trailer we pass has been partially crushed by a large fallen oak tree. The weight of the massive trunk and branches has crumpled it like a tin can. The yard is full of detritus indicating that a child lived there once: broken plastic tricycles, Barbie Dreamhouses, and popped Hoppity Hops. Then we see the smoke curling up from a stovepipe in the roof. Somebody still lives here.

The poverty in this area feels no different than the poverty in third-world countries. Oakley and I ride through, wide-eyed, and wonder aloud, "Why isn't somebody paying attention? Why aren't we helping? How have these hidden communities been so neglected?"

Deep in thought about the inequities and injustices in America, I hear a mewing sound coming from the side of the road. I look over and see that it is coming from a trash can sitting by the side of the road.

"Oakley, there is a cat in that can!" I shout.

He is cruising behind me and comes to an abrupt halt. This boy loves cats as if they were his brethren. He dashes over to the garbage can, and as he peers in, I can see his face contort with simultaneous joy and horror. "Mom! There are kittens in here! Two trash kittens!"

I drop my bike and already feel the dread of responsibility as I walk over to see. Sure enough, there are two sweet tabbies in the bottom of the bin. They seem to be about five or six weeks old. They look up at us, mewling and shaking. Oakley quickly swoops them up. "Mama, somebody was throwing these out!"

I try to deny the truth of this. "No, Oakley, they must have fallen in. Nobody would do that." But even as I speak, I know that it isn't true. Kittens can't climb up a three-foot-tall empty metal can and hurl themselves into the bottom.

"Mom, you know they did. We can't leave them here." He holds both the kittens in his hands and looks at me with pleading eyes. I picture stuffing them in our panniers, riding thirty-five miles with them to the next two-horse town, and bringing them to the police station, only to have the officer shrug and say, "Not my problem." It's upwards of eighty-five degrees, and our panniers are crammed full. Who even knows if the next town *has* a police station?

"Let's check in with the neighbors and see if they know anything."

We carry the kittens in our arms and walk to the surrounding homes. We are greeted at the first house by an elderly woman who looks as startled to see us standing in her yard as we were to see the kittens. We try to ask her if she knows her neighbors or anything about these kittens, but she just stares at me and shakes her head. I think she may be deaf.

At the next house we are told that they have never met any neighbors around here and that we should just leave the kittens be.

"They have no food or water, and they are too young to be outside," protests Oakley.

The man shrugs. "Sorry." He goes back inside.

Nobody answers at the third house, but we see a curtain flicker. We return to where we found the kittens and empty a water bottle into a Tupperware container we have. We place it on the porch.

"Oakley, we have to leave them."

"They will die!" objects Oakley. But even he realizes we can't take them, in part because we have no idea what we will encounter next, not the least of which may be dogs chasing our bikes, which will lustfully sniff out the tiny, tasty kitten morsels on our bikes.

"I am so sorry." Oakley sits and strokes them as they bound in and out of his lap. Finally, he resolutely stands up, places the cats between a bush and the front porch, and gets on his bike. He doesn't look back. He doesn't falter. He just rides fast. I follow, feeling sick and sorry. It is a cruel world.

When we stop for lunch, I text my family at home and send them a few pictures of what we call the Trash Kittens. They are met with judgment and horror.

"How could you?" scolds my twenty-one-year-old son.

"Go back and get them!" rebuffs my nineteen-year-old daughter.

"I can't believe you just left them to die," says my twenty-four-year-old son in disbelief. Is this really his vegetarian, wildlife-loving, hippie-like mother just letting suffering happen? Yes, it is. But what can we do? I feel guilty all over again and groan. Oakley meets my eyes.

"Mom, there was nothing we could do. They don't know. They are not here. They don't get it." And we sit on the side of the road, eating bananas on hot dog buns slathered in peanut butter.

That night we sidle into Fordsville, Kentucky. The maps that we carry identify places that welcome cyclists to spend the night. In this town, another local fire station has opened its doors. When we arrive, rain is beginning to pelt down, and we are pretty excited to get warm and dry. However, much to my dismay, there is a Baptist family reunion taking place in the fire truck bay. They are having a potluck and singing gospel songs in full Baptist glory. Oakley is eager to join the festivities, sure that we will be welcome to partake in the large bowls of macaroni salad, spongy dinner rolls, and Jell-O salads that cover several folding tables, but I am not in the mood for a religious singalong and instead sequester myself under someone's carport.

"Mom!" Oakley fumes as I busy myself making cucumber mayonnaise tortilla roll-ups for dinner. Sometimes you just can't.

When the family celebrations begin to wind down, I pull on my extrovert mask and wheel my bike over to the station. There are two firefighters left, and their wives are efficiently tidying up after the afternoon's festivities. They are well dressed in coiffed hair and fresh lipstick. We, on the other hand, are a sorry-looking pair: wet, dirty and exhausted, having worn the same clothes for literally months.

"Hi," I say feeling shy, homeless, and bereft. "We heard there might be somewhere we could stay around here?" And that is all it takes; southern kindness reigns again.

"What? Why of course!" booms a fireman with a big gray beard and honest-to-God red suspenders. "Come on in! Get out of the rain. Help yourself to some leftovers. Janice, leave that food out for a minute." The man looks at Oakley. "I bet you are starving. We are just getting ready to leave, but you are welcome to stay here. Let me show you around." He walks us through the station and shows us how the lights, television, stove, and showers work. Everything is polished to a level that only firefighters are capable of. "There are Cokes in the fridge, and I think some ice cream. Help yourselves. If the alarm goes off tonight, just get out of the way and turn out the lights when the trucks leave." Oakley and I are wide-eyed at this hospitality.

Janice, who I assume is his wife, checks in one more time. "Now, you two have a great night. Here is our number if you need anything."

And with that they leave, shutting the large bay doors behind them. And there we are, safe, warm, and dry in the heart of Kentucky. The yin and the yang of rural life. Oakley climbs all over the trucks, inspecting every switch and lever. We ogle the tidily outfitted cubbies that run the perimeter of the room, each complete with hats, rubber boots, and pants stored in such a way that one could put their feet in the boots and pull up the pants in one fell swoop. We shower in the immaculate bathroom decorated in shiny corrugated tin and fire-engine red. We set up our pads and sleeping bags next to our favorite big engine and watch movies on the big-screen television.

"See. And you were scared to come here," Oakley says.

"I wasn't scared, just shy," I say.

"Why? The people here are so nice!"

And he is right. Sleeping in a fire station is a boy's dream come true.

May 14, 2006

Oakley was three years old. The other children had a science fair at their elementary school. It was evening, and the school was packed with over one thousand parents and family members, all there to support their children and celebrate their accomplishments. The hallways were crowded, and we moved between classrooms elbow to elbow with a jostling herd.

"I will take Oakley," I offered to Twain, "and you take the others so that you can actually see something." After all, this was their classmates' work, and Oakley was not going to stay still long enough to let anybody focus their attention on anything but him.

"Okay," said Twain, happy for the reprise. They went one way, and I went the other. Mr. Squirmy was not a big fan of me holding him, and he wriggled uncomfortably in my arms. I couldn't just take him outside because it was dark out, so I put him down and tried to hold his hand. This didn't work either. There was way too much stimulation. He struggled to get out of my grasp, succeeded, and wriggled through the crowd. His small body wove and darted where I couldn't go without elbowing other parents to get by.

No matter, because we were coming to the end of the long hallway, and there was nowhere to go. I scanned the end just to be sure, given his history of running away. And that was when I saw it—the fire alarm—right at waist level, right within his reach. And I knew it. He had also seen it. And now there were ten people between us. And he was grinning, and his arm was outstretched, and I was stumbling forward. And there were six people, and his chubby hand was reaching up, and there were two, and my finger grazed his back but couldn't gain purchase, and his little fingers pulled down on that little white plastic bar. And with that, the lights in the hallways started to flash. And then the alarm sounded, penetratingly, repeatedly, horrifyingly.

I swept him up. "No, Oakley, no!"

But it was too late. The hallway filled with commotion as all the parents looked around quizzically and began herding themselves towards the exit. Crap! I had to stop this. All of these people would leave. The fire trucks would come. We would ruin the whole fair! I put my shoulder down and tried to hustle through the crowded hall, holding my squirmy overgrown baby. My only hope was to get to the principal's office as quickly as possible and tell them. Tell them it was a false alarm. Get them to turn it off. As I pushed my way through the crowd, people around me began to grow agitated and annoyed.

"Don't push," they scolded me. "We will all get out if we stay calm."

I was not calm. I was frantic.

After what seemed an eternity, I made it to the front office and nearly fell through the door. There stood the principal. I was flushed scarlet.

"Um, it was just . . . "

The principal cut me off. "Oh no, it was him?" he stated, more a fact than a question. (Oakley had a reputation that preceded him, I'm afraid.) He wasn't smiling, just grimly staring. "Well, it is too late now."

One, then two, then three fire trucks pulled up outside, their red lights cutting through the darkness, sirens blaring. The alarms were shut off as I left the building. Waiting there under the glow of the light were Twain and my other children. Twain shook his head. With one glance, he knew what he had already suspected.

"Let's get out of here," I mumbled. Oakley grinned and pointed with delight at the trucks and commotion around us. The other children were at once humiliated by his behavior and in awe at his audacity. A little proud, a little ashamed, but all those fire trucks? A boy's dream.

Oakley's Two Cents

Crazy Things

This week has a list of the three craziest things that have happened on the whole trip:

1. First, the dog update. The dogs here in Kentucky can be really scary, but if you stop your bike when they start chasing, they realize that you're a human and not a deer or something else exciting to chase. We have had a few scary moments where dogs have been pretty threatening to us, but we have never been bitten or had to spray a dog with our bear spray. Today we were going through a very quiet little town when a little party of dogs showed and followed us to the edge of town like a dog parade. They were barking their heads off the whole time. We have also noticed that

some dogs seem neglected and abused. People put their dogs in tight, stinky kennels and leave them there, or on chains, all day.

2. A couple days ago, we took a day off in Berea, Kentucky. We camped out behind a fire station, and the next morning we went to a café in the morning and spent the rest of the day at the library and walking around. Berea has a college where it is free for students, but they have to work for their tuition by making crafts and selling them. The money does not go to students; it goes to the school because they're paying off their tuition. Berea College is a super wealthy school. They say it's like Harvard. Anyway, on the morning of our departure from Berea, we heard that there was a murder and kidnapping suspect at large in the next county that we happened to be biking through. They closed all the schools. My mom did not know what to do, but we figured that the man would be hiding, not wandering around seeking bikers to kill, so we went for it. It was stressful.

3. On the same day we were worrying about the murder suspect, we were biking down the road, and I passed a trash can that had meows coming from it. I quickly turned back and got off my bike to look into the trash can. Looking up at me were two trapped, stupid-cute kittens. I could not believe my eyes. The two kittens looked at me with their beautiful, blue eyes and meowed. I scooped them up and showed them to my mom. We couldn't figure out whether the people were trying to get rid of them or they just got stuck in the trash can. It was so heartbreaking to leave the babies behind, but there was nothing else we could do.

The Quests That Never End

October 19–25, 2019

Virginia

It seems like overnight it has gone from summer to fall. Where we used to fear the heat, now we seek it. With the cool temperatures has come rain. As Oakley and I begin to navigate the Appalachian Mountains, we are treated to a wide range of weather conditions on an hourly basis.

Mornings are cool and damp and involve rolling up dewy tents and eating breakfast standing up so we don't get wet tuchuses. Then comes the age-old question: Do we wear rain gear today or not? If we wear it, we will get hot—really hot—as we huff and puff over these mountains. If we don't, we will get wet and chilled within the first few minutes of our day and then have to deal with sodden bike shorts and shirts potentially for days. Then there is sliding your feet into wet sneakers—another joy. Luckily, as we continue to pedal eastward, the opportunities to stay in firehouses, churches, and hostels increase, and we are welcomed into many warm dry refuges at day's end.

But not today. Today we are caught off guard by the relentlessness of the Appalachian Mountains. It is only thirty-eight degrees when we head out in the morning, and it isn't long before the rain soaks us through. We ride for seventy-one miles before we get to our campsite. It is aptly named Look Out Town Campsite and is situated on top of a hill that has a seventeen-percent grade. Oakley is foul. He curses me. He curses this trip.

When we finally get to the apex of this mount, I decide to break our routine and feed him before he sets up the tent. He is looking particularly rangy, much like a rabid dog, and it seems imperative that I quell his rage lest I get bit.

First I give him a jar of peanut butter. He eats it with a spoon. Then a sheaf of crackers, a jar of applesauce, spaghetti, some cut-up veggies, and three protein bars. He lays back on the bench of the picnic table and stares at the trees overhead. "I feel great!" he says.

Feeding Oakley has been a monstrous task. He needs an exorbitant number of calories. Often he eats four solid meals a day plus an entire box of protein bars or Pop-Tarts or Lance peanut butter crackers. Sometimes he travels with an open jar of Nutella in his handlebar bag and scoops it out with a spoon as he pedals. He never tells me when he eats as we cycle because he doesn't want to draw attention to it and risk my scorn. Instead I see the evidence of his constant feasting in endless wrappers stuffed in every crevice of his bags. Every day, I let him buy a family-sized box of snacks of his choice as an addition to our shared snacks and meals, and I never expect to see them again.

Nutrition has also been a huge issue. From Oregon to Virginia, it feels as though we have been in a food desert. We have subsisted nearly entirely on dollar-store and convenience-store food. Everything has been heavily processed, and most of the ingredients we cannot pronounce. Our menu mostly consists of True Value macaroni and cheese, instant oatmeal, tortillas wrapped around cheese or peanut butter or Nutella, granola bars, and spaghetti. Sometimes we are lucky enough to get rice and beans, but not often. There is rarely anything fresh except for the odd cucumber or apple. It is a wonder how people who live in rural America don't have scurvy.

When we started this journey, Oakley loved our diet and was like a kid in the proverbial candy store when he saw our food selection because much of it is taboo in our household. All the junk he has always wanted—this has been our only option. There have been few grocery stores along our route because that route has taken us on almost all back roads, far from large towns and all their accompanying goods and services. When we do happen upon one, we can only buy supplies for a day or two because we have no refrigeration and limited carrying capacity. And within a month, even Oakley grew sick of the options and would fantasize about salads and fruit.

Now we have reached a level where we eat just to fuel our bodies. Calories in, power out. It has ceased to be about taste. Oakley's body is showing it. His acne is terrible, and he is skinny. I relish the thought of fattening him up when we get home.

We arrive in Damascus, Virginia. This town is famous for being the hub of several crisscrossing trails. The Appalachian Trail passes through as well as the TransAmerica Trail. There are hundreds of miles of mountain biking trails here and the longest rail trail in North America: a thirty-five-mile, two-percent downhill grade called the Virginia Creeper Trail. People come from all around to play, and the culture is sporty and festive. As Oakley and I pull in, we decide to take advantage of one of the many hostels in the area set up to serve through-hikers and bikers. I ask at the tourism office for the least expensive one and am directed to Crazy Larry's Hostel.

When we have pulled into the yard and are locking our bikes up outside, we hear a voice call out to us from the front porch of the old parsonage-turned-hostel: "Are you Leah and Oakley?" We spin about. "I knew you were coming!" calls a man wearing a green Appalachian Mountain Club shirt, flip-flops, and quick-dry hiking shorts.

"Um, yes, that's us," I respond, feeling a bit mystified and uneasy.

"I have been reading your blog as you crossed the country!" The man grins. "I knew you would stop here; I could tell you were getting close. Welcome." Oakley and I feel both proud and uncomfortable. We are pretty used to being anonymous and shift uneasily under this man's attention. I have been writing a blog about our adventure titled "Bikemum." It has helped to make sense out of what we were doing and to feel the virtual support of a community of enthusiastic family and friends. I sort of felt it was just going out into space, but now I feel that we are supposed to live up to something in this man's eyes, and I am not sure we have what it takes.

Oakley is pretty sick of living a book and having to recount things through journaling and blogging, and now answering questions seems like work. The man means well, but we both want to just be tired and dirty and as cranky as we desire. In the morning, we awaken to a downpour. We have a choice: stay in the hostel for the morning or hightail it into the storm. Oakley picks the storm, and off we go.

We climb and climb and soar and soar up and over the last of the Appalachians. It is getting colder by the day, so we don hats and bike gloves. Our strength is astounding now, even to me, and I notice that our average daily mileage, regardless of the unstable weather, is now routinely over sixty-five miles. One day, we decide to take a shortcut and miss a detour sign. We ride downhill for eight miles to a river with no bridge, shrug, and turn around and head back up to where we went wrong. It is no longer a catastrophe, just a minor inconvenience.

I feel as though Oakley and I have been journeying side by side on three different epic quests during this bicycling adventure: a quest to see and understand the world better, personal internal quests to see what we are made of, and a family quest to navigate our parent-child relationship in a healthy way.

The first quest has been the most enjoyable: experiencing the deserts, the small towns, the magnificent rivers, the wildlife, and the people—all strikingly different and strikingly the same.

We have learned how the land across the United States is shaped and how this land holds different ecosystems that all encompass their own worlds pressing up against each other and mixing together along the edges. There are little connections between these worlds of migrating animals and flowing waterways, but for the most part they are separate and distinct and change from one hour to the next as we pedal through. There is a startling amount of variety in life and landscape in this country.

We have also been lucky enough to interact with all manner of people within this diverse landscape and see how those people seem to mimic the land around them: the leathery, tough desert dwellers; the quiet, hidden people living in the hollows between shady hills; and the expansive warmth of the prairie dwellers.

We have found that most everyone is kind if given the opportunity, no matter their ideologies or lifestyles. When we have needed help, it has always been there. We have had lunch paid for by strangers, rides given to bike shops when our bikes have broken down, ice-cold bottles of water and snacks handed to us as we cycle by, offers of lodging and money, and countless cheers, thumbs-up, and friendly honks. It has been incredible to experience this support and generosity, both from friends at home and from perfect strangers. It really, truly does fuel us.

The second quest is a dual quest. Though we are together in our journey, we have our own personal physical, mental, and emotional quests. We process and respond to our journey in our own ways. This trip has been incredibly demanding physically and, at times, emotionally. The hills have been huge, the winds fierce, the dogs scary, and the feeling of not knowing what the next day may hold is exhausting. We have had to push ourselves farther than we ever have. We have had to fling ourselves into the unknown over and over. I know a lot of people have successfully completed a bike tour across America with panache, but for me it has been deeply challenging. I have also been homesick and longed for my husband, my other children, my dog, and the safety and security of my own bed.

Oakley has had his own challenges to overcome, and this trip has made him confront his issues with impulsivity, delayed gratification, and anger on a daily basis. He also has had to step away from peers and social media and the support that can often be found there, for better and for worse. He has left behind all predictability and routine in his life and has had to trust his own abilities and take on the world without the comforts found in his hometown.

I am interested to see how this shapes us.

The third quest has been a mother-son relationship quest. Spending twelve weeks with my sixteen-year-old son in such an intense way has been a psychological trip unto itself. Oakley struggles to understand the ramifications of his actions; he can be irrational; he lives solely in the present and does not always follow the rules. He needs perpetual forgiveness and support, and sometimes that feels beyond my abilities. He still carries his Tide Pods, which we have never used. And he still begs to be treated like a man.

As for Oakley, I am sure he would tell you that I drive him crazy as well. I am a nag. I am uptight and probably pretty boring. However, nearly every day he expresses his affections and his gratitude that I am by his side. I know he sees that we are a team, even during the hard times. We still have so much to work out, but I think the lessons we have learned on this trip will shape how we relate to one another for the rest of our lives. I crave adult company, but I will miss him like crazy when we have to reintegrate the rest of our loved ones into our relationship.

August 10, 2006

It was a warm autumn afternoon, and I had deluded myself into thinking that it was a good idea to walk through a corn maze outside Charleston, South Carolina, with my four young children. Oakley is three and a half. I know better, but I want a normal life.

The maze is on a farm and has other attractions that I think all my children will enjoy. There is a hayride, a pumpkin patch, and a goat exhibit. The goat exhibit is really quite something. It is comprised of a three-story playground (of sorts) with narrow planks ascending to a feeding platform forty feet high. It is fascinating to watch the goats mince their way up the boards to such a great height with complete confidence and coordination.

After we watch them for a bit, we hit the maze. We turn left, then right, then left again through the tall corn. Suddenly I notice that Oakley is missing. (You saw that coming, didn't you?) But, this time, just as I notice he is gone, I hear a woman's shriek—"That is a baby up there!"—and I know just where he is. What do I feel? Embarrassment? Fear? Resignation? I try to herd my children in the direction of the goat display. It takes some time—it is a maze, after all.

When we arrive, there is Oakley. He has climbed the enclosure's fence and scrabbled up those narrow planks to the very top of the structure. He is standing by the feeding platform, beaming. A firefighter is below him, coaxing Oakley into his arms. I am humiliated. I have to step forward. "He is with me." I feel the spectator's eyes burn into me as I wait for the firefighter to gingerly carry him down and place him in my arms, and I wonder if I am cut out for a child like this. He is so much, but is he too much?

Oakley grasps my face in his chubby hands. His long blond ringlets bounce on his shoulders, his eyes dance, and his ruddy cheeks glow. He grins wickedly like a mischievous cupid. "Are you proud of me?" he asks.

And I am. I wish I could have gotten away with that feat. I think we all do, but I also feel a constriction in my chest. How am I going to do this?

Today, I still feel the same way. I am amazed by Oakley's vibrancy and with his skills. Despite his chronic misbehavior, I believe that if I can keep being proud of him, and more importantly that he can keep being proud of himself, we will make it through. He still makes my heart feel tight, but I wouldn't trade him for an instant. He is not too much. He is just enough.

October 21, 2019

After we climb Mount Vesuvius, we continue along the ridge of the Blue Ridge Parkway as the rain intensifies, and an icy wind picks up. Before long we find ourselves pedaling through a thick cloud cover as well, and visibility is reduced to thirty feet or so. Oakley bikes ahead of me, and every minute or so I lose sight of him, causing me to call, again and again, "You're losing me!" If I can't see him, neither can the driver of a car coming up behind us. I feel both our anxiety levels rising.

"Mom!" shouts Oakley. "This isn't safe!" He is right, but we don't have many options. Now that we are on the ridgeline, there are not many access points to get off. I take out my tiny map and scan it for the hundredth time for a nearby town as rain pelts down, freezing my fingers.

"Look, Oakley, just five more miles, and it looks like there is a resort. We can stop there and get some lunch and get dried out!"

We continue on, becoming colder and colder until we get to the so-called resort, only to find it doesn't exist; instead there is only a deeply rutted dirt road leading into a soggy field.

"Mom, what are you talking about? There is no town!" yells Oakley. Fear always makes him angry.

How could it be? It was there on the map, I swear! I take out the maps again. There is no sign of the town on the maps now. I must have been willing there to be a town to such an extent that my hope deluded me like an oasis in the desert.

I feel a deeper chill seep into my bones. My fingers are clumsy and distant. And I begin to realize that we might be in trouble. "Let's hitch-hike off the parkway. We got up. That was the hard part. Now let's just get down any way we can!"

We put our bikes to the side of the road and stick out our thumbs.

Minutes pass with not a single car. I begin jumping up and down on the side of the road and pace in a frenzied manner.

"What is your problem?" questions Oakley.

"I am too cold, Oakley, really."

"I am cold too."

"No, Oakley, I am really too cold. I am dangerously cold." Oakley looks at me and assesses the situation. This is a new role for him, and I watch as his attitude shifts from being a grumpy teenager to realizing that he needs to put his own issues second and care for me. My chest feels hollow, and I feel pale and weak, like a skeleton with skin stretched across it.

"We need to get off this mountain now," he says. His voice is strong and steady. We anxiously peer into the fog, staring hard, hoping to see the glimmer of a headlight. Nobody is up here on such a miserable day; it seems we have the whole parkway to ourselves. Minutes tick by.

"I don't know what to do, Oakley," I mutter, feeling hypothermic stupidity begin to dull my brain. The wind sucks more and more warmth from me, making me less capable of clear decision making.

"Let's get on our bikes and ride, until we find a way down. We can't just stand here," says Oakley. He jumps on his bike and expects me to follow. I do. There is no mother-and-son team now, just two people relying on each other.

Oakley is the first to spot a loaded pickup truck on the side of the road.

"Mom, go tell them we need a ride."

I pull up along the driver's-side window and knock. A bearded man peers out at me in confusion through fogged glass. He quickly rolls down the window, and the warm air from the inside of the truck floods out and cascades down my face and shoulders.

"I am really cold," I stammer. "Can we have a ride off the mountain?"

The man begins moving as he speaks, opening the door and taking the bike from my hands. "Get inside. It is thirty miles to the closest town. I am not going that way, but I don't mind. It is too cold to be up here." He stands in the freezing rain in a T-shirt and jeans and quickly begins loading up our gear.

"I can help load our bikes," I stammer.

"Get in the truck," he says again. Oakley and I climb into the cab. It is warm and dry, and the seats feel like pillows. I never want to leave. The man detaches our panniers and stuffs them in the various dog cages that fill the back of his truck. He hoists our bikes on top and ties everything up. By the time he gets back in the truck, he is as wet as we are.

As we drive off the mountain, I do my best to make small talk. He is a bear hunter. He has three college-aged kids of his own. He loves camping and wants to go to Alaska. He repairs air conditioners for a living. The whole time he speaks, I sit with my arms wrapped tightly around my chest and my helmet on in case it might add to my warmth. I am afraid I might create a draft if I move at all. Suddenly, on the side of the road we see a bear. He is just sitting there on his haunches, scratching his ear in the rain. The man slows to a stop, and we just stare. It is the first bear Oakley and I have seen on our trip. I feel like it is the bear of all our fears saying goodbye.

After about a half an hour the truck driver drops us at a tiny gas station. Even though he has added an hour to his day and ended up soaking wet because of us, he thanks us for making his day. I thank him for perhaps saving my life.

Safe at last in the mini convenience store, I consume two Honey Buns and a package of Lance peanut butter crackers with my helmet still on. The clerk stares at us curiously, but we are beyond caring.

Oakley and I find a campground two miles farther down the road. The shop warmed me up a little, but it is still a miserable ride. The wind instantly chills me again. When we finally stagger into the campground office, I look and feel a mess. "Do you have tent sites?" I ask. The woman at the desk looks at me with concern.

"You were biking in this?" she asks incredulously.

Oakley leans into the conversation and proudly proclaims, "We are biking across the country, and we are almost done!"

"No kidding! Why don't you wait to set up your tent until it stops raining? We have video games in there, and a fire in here." She leads Oakley to an arcade game, much to his delight, and leads me into a quiet room with a roaring fire, complete with two big leather armchairs and footstools. "Dry out here. I will be right back."

She disappears, and I take off my shoes and socks and hang them on the fire screen. I change out of my sodden clothes and realize that my rain gear has leaked terribly. I scooch one of the chairs up to the fire and press my feet as close to it as I dare. When the woman returns, she is holding a steaming cup of coffee in one hand and a box of donuts in the other. "Here you go, ma'am. Take your time and just warm up."

Once again, for the hundredth time on our journey, I am amazed by the kindness of strangers. The cold in my chest is replaced by a warmth, and not just from the fire and coffee. People are good. They truly are. The campground owner on the other side of Mount Vesuvius, the bear hunter, this campground host—they all sandwiched our day in between so much care that I again have that sensation that we really aren't alone out here, not at all.

Oakley comes bopping back into this cozy little room while I sit there awash in all this good feeling. "Can I have some quarters for another game?"

"Absolutely," I answer. In that moment I would give him anything he asks. I think I can spare a few quarters.

Oakley's Two Cents

Things I Will Miss about This Trip:

1. The beautiful landscapes and passing fields of cows over and over
2. Sleeping outside and hearing everything outside the tent,

such as the bone-chilling cry of a lone coyote

3. Camping in random places such as city parks, fire stations, etc.

4. Passing over a mountain or state line and seeing the whole landscape change in front of my eyes

5. Looking at the map of the United States and marking off the places we have gone through and seeing how much more we have left

6. Staying at city parks and meeting other teenagers my age to fool around with and cause trouble

7. Riding up alongside endless freight trains . . . unless we are sleeping next to them and then NOT enjoying them at night coming and going every five minutes

8. Going to bed under the night sky full of stars

9. Scaring the heck out of wildlife while I bike by

10. Chilling at my campsite after a big day of riding

Things That I Will Not Miss from This Trip:

1. The headwinds in Kansas and the Rockies

2. The worries about bears in Yellowstone

3. The intense Rocky Mountains and Ozarks that just go up and up, over and over

4. People in cars slowing down when we are riding up a big hill and telling us that it is all uphill from there

5. The overloaded trucks that seem to just about almost kill us every time they pass

6. People trying to tell us we are too late in the season to try to bike across country

7. Missing home

8. The DOGS in Kentucky that chased us!

9. Roads that go straight up and don't have switchbacks

10. Only talking to my mom for three months straight!

On the last evening of our adventure, Oakley and I camp on the side of the James River, thirty miles from the finish line at Yorktown. We make a fire and sit up talking about our highs and lows and appreciating each other's strengths on the trip. This is Oakley's idea, and he begs to sleep under the stars next to the dying embers. We do. In the morning, the sun rises over the river, turning the early fog pink.

"Come on, Mom. Get up, let's go!" calls Oakley.

I sit up slowly and gaze about, feeling quieted by the magnitude of this day. Oakley has never woken me up before. Suddenly, we both hear a roaring clatter coming toward us. Is it a military jet? A huge powerboat? We freeze and peer in the direction of the sound. "What the . . . ?" questions Oakley, a little on edge.

All at once the sky fills with birds. Thousands of grackles descend on our campsite. Truly, thousands. More than I have ever seen. The cacophony they make is so loud that we have to shout over them, which we do, sharing our disbelief at their numbers and noise.

The grackles oust a couple of hawks and a handful of turkey vultures that begin circling overhead. A young raccoon goes scurrying across our campsite and dives into a hole halfway up an oak tree right next to our picnic table. The grackle party goes on and on. It is a madhouse. We pack up while this symphony is underway. It is like fireworks. It is like a party. It is the perfect send-off, and I have tears again.

Off we go, only thirty miles to Yorktown, Virginia—the end of our trip. We ride slowly, taking a pit stop in Williamsburg for a muffin and a cup of coffee.

"Okay, Oakley, let's go home," I say as we straddle our bikes for the last time.

My head and heart are full of so many complicated emotions that I am in a bit of a fog. Now we should only have ten miles to go, and I let go of my hypervigilance about checking and rechecking the map and instead become lulled into complacency. I expect the Atlantic Ocean to call us to its shores. My thoughts loop and circle about the magnitude of what we are about to accomplish and what awaits us at home. As we ride, the roads from Williamsburg seem to loop and circle as well, and, as might have been predicted, we get lost. Really lost. We find ourselves on busy cloverleaves, crushing intersections, and roads that seem to go to nowhere. Oakley begins to lose it and yells at me, venting all his frustrations and anxieties. I try to calmly coordinate our tiny maps with my phone's GPS, but once again I feel my blood pressure escalate. I have been catapulted from my quiet reverie back into reality. It is then that I realize that this trip isn't over. Maybe it will never be. We are both just regular people finding our way, with our strengths and our weakness guiding us.

After a little four-mile scenic loop, we do find the way, and Oakley and I continue on. As the last few miles take us along the coast, we look out and see sailboats and tankers navigating the sea. Then, suddenly, the Yorktown Victory Monument, which marks the end of the TransAmerica Trail, heaves into view. We ride up to it and reach out our hands to touch it. Its history marks a victory that is not ours, but nevertheless, it seems fitting.

We hug and grin and take pictures and push our bikes down to the ocean to dip our tires in the water as the tradition of cross-country riders calls for, but it is obvious we both feel a little lost. All there is to do now is to stop in at the Yorktown visitor center to register our arrival and call an Uber.

We stroll to the center and stand in line behind a group of tourists visiting this historic site. The park ranger in full ranger garb and matching hat is barking out directions to the group about driving and parking. We stand a little removed, both lost in thought and waiting our turn. Suddenly she is barking at us.

"If you don't pay attention, you will never know where to go, and

I am not going to repeat myself again!" She looks harassed and tired from a busy tourist season.

Quietly, I tell her that actually we don't need driving directions, but rather we have just biked across country and would like to sign the register.

"Oh my, I am sorry. Have a pin!" And she hands us a dime-sized pin of the state of Virginia. Oakley and I look at each other and smile. A pin. We got a pin, and it was all worth it. Should I say, *And I think we deserved it?*

Oakley's Two Cents

I Really Just Biked across the Country

Our last night on the road, we stayed at a campsite on a peninsula on the James River. That night in some ways was really sad and really happy. My mother and I sat by the fire and talked about our highs and lows of the trip and what we appreciated about biking across country. We both agreed that we appreciated how people were so nice and helpful to us. People would offer to fix our bikes. Someone paid for our meal one day. Everywhere we went, people were always trying to help us in some way.

The next morning at our lovely campsite, we were eating a breakfast of granola and milk and coffee when a huge swarm of grackles flew into the trees above us and all started chirping to each other. It was so loud that they started to stir up other animals, such as a raccoon, some hawks, and some other creatures.

I didn't really accept that we were done with the trip until the next morning, the day after arriving at my grandma's house. When I woke the next morning, I got up and thought to myself, *I really just biked across the country.* Even in the car right now, two days later and on the way back home to Maine, I still can't believe it.

Now that I am literally on my way home, I think about all the adventures that I've had, and I would like to thank my mother for making me bike across America and go through all the hard times together. I wouldn't have been able do this on my own.

Thank you, Mom.

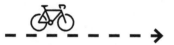

Twain is driving Oakley and me up the New Jersey Turnpike toward home. A heavy rain is rattling against the roof of the car, and every few minutes we hydroplane just a little. My knees and elbows ache. I have calloused palms embedded with gravel. I have lost twenty pounds. Other than that, there is no indication that Oakley and I have just completed a 4,329-mile ride across the United States.

It has only been three days since we coasted to a stop in Yorktown, Virginia, but already I ache to get back on our bikes and see what is around the next corner. Watching the land unfold before us, meeting kind strangers at every stop, and focusing our days on the simplest of needs—food, rest, shelter, and working together—helped life make sense. Now these billboards I see out the car window—advertising XXX Erotica at exit 8 and the Honda Car Dealership at exit 7—seem especially crass and off-putting.

Today, I feel pulled in many directions. I am longing to see my home and family, beginning to think about what the next phase of my life is going to look like, and already missing our adventure terribly. How is this possible?

Oakley has been very affectionate since we finished biking, and there is a deep feeling of camaraderie between us. I feel pangs of worry that this bond will soon become diluted when we get caught up in our respective lives, but maybe not. Maybe our bond will settle deep within and become the substrate for dealing with future challenges and teenage transitions that we will soon be facing.

This trip has taught us an incredible amount about ourselves, our abilities, the world, people, and how they all entwine. It has taught us that the best things come from allowing ourselves to be a bit uncomfortable, a bit scared, and a bit reckless.

It occurs to me as I head home that this adventure, this book, and this life that I am living are all a love letter. A love letter to Oakley and to life: the people, the places, the vibrancy, the challenges, the beauty, all of which are teaching me so much, every day. I will never be able to thank enough everyone who has supported us along the way. The kindness we have experienced has been astounding. This world can be a beautiful place.

Afterword

November 10, 2019

It has been a little more than two weeks since Oakley and I returned from our bike journey across the United States. We are gradually reassimilating into our community, our responsibilities, and our routines. But we are not the same. Our bicycle adventure feels like it has changed the lenses through which we see.

Speaking for myself, I feel ten years younger. I have energy and enthusiasm that I have not felt since I was thirty. I feel as though if you could peek beneath my skin, instead of blood and guts you would find the fields of Kansas with golden oats blowing in the wind under a clear blue sky. You would find the clear rivers tumbling down from the Cascade Mountains in Oregon. You would find the sound of coyotes yipping and yodeling under the Wyoming night sky. You would find a stranger offering me shelter, a cup of coffee, and a donut in Kentucky and warming up my heart and belly with food and courage.

As for Oakley, he too is changed. He told me this weekend that he felt that people were treating him like he was an adult lately, and it made him want to act like one. A neighbor stopped my husband and me on a walk this morning and commented that the biggest change she sees in Oakley, aside from his stature, confidence, and strength, is that he doesn't seem twitchy anymore. He is contained and relaxed and moves with ease and composure. It is true. There is an inner calm in him.

A few times since our return, Oakley has needed a reminder that his behavior is becoming too intense. At these points, I separated him from others and was able to have calm conversations with him: "Is this how you want to be?" or "Remember on our trip how we did it differently?" He does remember. And he does regroup without becoming deregulated. He wants this. He knows how good it feels to be in control and be granted adult status.

The other day Oakley and I went for a walk to check in with each other. We talked all about the trip. We talked about how being home is sometimes overstimulating. I told him I would do it again next summer if I could, and he said he would do it again when he was thirty. I guess I didn't scar him for life after all.

I wish everybody could have a reboot such as ours every once in a while. Now I face trying to re-create a career and find ways to dig us out of the financial pit that our bike trip created. Yesterday, my husband and I sat down at the kitchen table and analyzed the train wreck of our finances. But I don't feel overwhelmed. I feel like there are endless possibilities, and if I just stay open to them, it will all work out.

This Thursday, Oakley and I are giving a slideshow about our trip at the local community center. I absolutely detest public speaking, but it seems important to share our tale with everybody who supported us. I will be an uncomfortable, jittery mess, but if I can bike across the country, I can do this. I can do a lot that I never thought I could.

Appendix

Statistics

- Elevation gain—219,855 feet (Mount Everest is only 29,032 feet)
- Distance—4,329 miles
- Length of time—84 days
- Highest mileage in a day—88 miles
- Average mileage—56
- Days off—6
- Hitchhiked—124 miles, bringing total distance to 4,363 miles
- Other cross-country cyclists seen—13
- Got lost—4 times, adding 51 miles to trip
- Dog attacks—1
- Bear attacks—0

Places We Slept

- 7 hotel rooms
- 6 hostels
- 5 fire stations
- 3 churches
- 23 city parks
- 13 state and national parks
- 13 private campgrounds
- 2 Lions Clubs
- 1 American Legion
- 1 Elks Club
- 9 RV parks
- 1 highway rest area

Bike Repairs

- 2 flat tires
- 12 broken spokes
- 1 replaced wheel
- 2 replaced brakes
- 2 derailleur adjustments
- 2 replaced chains
- 3 abandoned fenders
- 1 broken pannier rack
- 1 replaced, worn-through Kevlar tire
- 1 broken odometer

(All fixed in five bike shops along the way in Oregon, Montana, Colorado, Kansas, and Virginia)

Most Common Foods

- Oreos
- ramen
- macaroni and cheese
- beans and rice
- Honey Buns
- Nutella
- applesauce
- salad in a bag
- instant oatmeal
- Pop-Tarts
- Lance peanut butter crackers
- bagels
- grits
- canned fruit
- protein bars
- cheese sticks
- yogurt

Bike Shops That Helped Us Get Started

- Brad's Bike Rental and Repair, Peaks Island, Maine (advice, fixes, moral support, solid friendship, corny jokes)
- Allspeed Cyclery and Snow, Portland, Maine (bike boxes and good cheer)
- Gear Hub, Portland, Maine (built our bikes despite our "help")

Towns and Places: Night 1 through Night 84

Start: Astoria, OR (bike shop: Bikes & Beyond)

1. Fort Stevens State Park (coastal Oregon)—enormous beautiful trees with beards of Spanish moss standing side by side with endless golden, sandy beaches
2. Manzanita, Neahkahnie, and Nehalem State Parks, Nehalem, OR (coastal Oregon) (Cannon Beach; Haystack Rock)—caves on the beach with beautiful campgrounds tucked among the dunes and majestic trees overlooking the sea
3. Cape Lookout State Park, Tillamook, OR, with stops at Sand Lake Recreation Area and Sand Lake Dunes—huge dunes by the sea, perfect for flipping and sliding, with tidepools full of treasure
4. Grand Ronde, OR
5. Independence, OR—a charming town along the Willamette River
6. Armitage Park, Eugene, OR (Willamette Valley) (Bike shop: Peak Sports Bike Shop)

7. Belknap Hot Springs, McKenzie, OR (McKenzie River, part of National Wild & Scenic Rivers System)—cannonball contest, natural medicinal soaks

8. Sisters, OR (over McKenzie Pass) (Mt. Washington Wilderness; Three Sisters; Belknap Lava Crater; Mt. Washington; Dee Wright Observatory)—unbelievable geological wonders; 360-degree views of snowcapped peaks, lava fields, and fertile valleys

9. REST DAY: Sisters, OR (Paulina Springs Books)

10. Ochoco Lake State Park, OR

11. Spoke'n Hostel, Mitchell, OR (Painted Desert; Ochoco Pass)—the kindest man ever and his wife run this hostel surrounded by the painted hills—thank you!

12. Mt. Vernon, OR (John Day Valley; petroglyphs at Clyde Holliday State Recreation Site)—we found petroglyphs by the side of the river

13. Prairie City, OR (Bates State Park) (Strawberry Mountain, Monument Rock)—a high mountain western town, set back in time, the cleanest air

14. Baker City, OR (bike shop: The Trailhead; Betty's Books; National Historic Oregon Trail Interpretive Center)—great Mexican food, and the Oregon Trail museum should not be missed

15. Oxbow, OR (Oxbow Campground; Wallowa Mountains; Snake River, part of National Wild & Scenic Rivers System; Hells Canyon)—oasis in the bottom of the canyon

16. Cambridge, ID (Mundo Hot Springs)—natural hot spring swimming pools

17. New Meadows, ID

18. White Bird, ID (Hoots Café) (Salmon River, part of the National Wild & Scenic Rivers System; Frank Church–River of No Return)— awesome meat lover's pizza and a beautiful car-free mountain pass

19. Kooskia, ID—Has there ever been a hotter town?

20. Wilderness Gateway, ID (Clearwater River, part of the National

Wild & Scenic Rivers System; Nez Perce Reservation; South Fork Campground)—incredible, clear, majestic river

21. Lochsa Lodge, ID (Lolo Pass)—where Lewis and Clark passed into Idaho—you can feel those that came before here

22. Missoula, MT (Adventure Cycling headquarters—provided maps for our journey; Shady Spruce Hostel)—great outdoor summer music festival

23. REST DAY: Missoula, MT

24. Darby, MT (bike shop: Valley Bicycles; Payette National Forest, over Lost Trail Pass and Bitterroot Mountains, crossing Continental Divide for first time)—I cried a lot because my bicycle broke, but the ride up into the Rockies for the first time from here was worth it

25. Wisdom, MT (Beaverhead Historic Site; Deerlodge National Forest; Big Hole National Battlefield)—my favorite place, filled with lowing cattle, chortling coyotes, and frost on the tall grass in August

26. Dillon, MT (bike shop)—professor of outdoor education at Montana State University, had a bike shop in his garage, fixed our wobbly wheels

27. Virginia City, MT (Old West Victorian town)—old Western town with wooden sidewalks

28. Earthquake Lake, MT—powerful story of loss in this beauty

29. West Yellowstone, MT (bike shop: Yellowstone Bicycle)—bought bear spray

30. Grant Village, WY (Yellowstone National Park)—my bike was christened "Rocinante" by a fellow TransAmerica cyclist and now friend

31. Colter Bay, WY (Grand Tetons)—beauty stopped us in our tracks

32. Hatchet Creek, WY (Jackson Lake; Bridger-Teton National Forest; Togwotee Mountain Lodge)—fields of alpine flowers, red, orange, purple, blue, and gold—and plenty of grizzlies

33. Dubois, WY (St. Thomas' Episcopal Church lets cyclists stay the night—thank you!)—Dubois is also the land of the jackalope

34. Lander, WY (Wind River Range; bike shop: Gannett Peak Sports)—cycled through impoverished reservations and an outdoor adventurer mecca

35. Jeffrey City, WY (Sweetwater Station)—uranium mine ghost town

36. Saratoga, WY (Hobo Hot Springs, Saratoga Lake Campground, bike shop: Rawlins Outdoor Shop; O'Reilly Auto Parts)—Oakley's favorite day

37. REST DAY: Saratoga, WY (Hobo Hot Springs; Saratoga Lake Campground)

38. Encampment, WY (Six Mile Gap; Medicine Bow)

39. Walden, CO (Arapaho and Roosevelt National Forests)

40. Hot Sulphur Springs, CO

41. Breckenridge, CO (bike shops: Pioneer Sports, Silverthorne, CO; Elevation Ski & Bike, Breckenridge, CO; The Bivvi Hostel in Breckenridge; Old Dillon Reservoir Trailhead; Cucumber Gulch Wildlife Preserve; Sapphire Point Overlook)—highest pass—Hoosier Pass

42. Cañon City, CO (Mosquito Range; Mt. Democrat; Hoosier Ridge; Royal Gorge)—Oakley almost gets hit by a truck

43. Pueblo, CO (Lake Pueblo State Park)—campgrounds full, turned away, so many gophers

44. Ordway, CO—sirens at eight o'clock signifying people must be in their homes

45. Eads, CO

46. Tribune, KS—where all wind is born, I believe

47. Scott City, KS—the wind—you will never forget the wind or the skies that go on forever but hold you all at once

48. Alexander, KS (bike shop: Golden Belt Bicycle Co.; Grass Prairie Reservation; Quivira National Wildlife Refuge)—six-foot-tall prairie grass

49. Nickerson, KS—the town center is comprised of rows upon rows of silos and grain bins

50. Newton, KS—Twain came

51. Cassoday, KS—I am sick, and the water tastes like oil. Was it beautiful? Yes.

52. Toronto, KS (Fall River State Park)

53. Chanute, KS

54. REST DAY: Chanute, KS

55. Girard, KS

56. Golden City, MO (Cooky's Café & Pie)—there is pie for breakfast, over twenty choices!

57. Fair Grove, MO

58. Hartville, MO—the tent kitten

59. Summersville, MO—the hardest hills

60. Ellington, MO (Ozark Scenic Riverways)—more of the hardest hills!

61. Farmington, MO (Bike hostel: Al's Place)—a Shangri-La of bike hostels

62. Chester, IL—Popeye's birthplace, crossed Mississippi River

63. Carbondale, IL (Little Grassy Lake State Park; Crab Orchard National Wildlife Refuge)

64. Rosiclare, KY (Cave-in-Rock State Park; Ohio River; Fluorspar Festival)—slept along the banks of the Ohio River

65. Sebree, KY (Amish country)—we passed children driving buggies full of their friends to school in the cool morning fog

66. Fordsville, KY (Baptist Church—thank you!)

67. White Mills, KY (firehouse—thank you!)

68. Springfield, KY (firehouse—thank you!)

69. Berea, KY (Berea College)—a place to get a latte and ogle beautiful crafts in a lovely town

70. REST DAY: Berea, KY

71. Booneville, KY—parades of friendly dogs

72. Hindman, KY

73. Breaks Interstate Park, VA

74. Council, VA (Council Park)

75. Damascus, VA (bike shop: Bicycle Junction, near Appalachian Trail; Virginia Creeper Trail; hostel: The Place)—junction of many biking and hiking trails creates a dynamic outdoor mecca here

76. Wytheville, VA—the Appalachian Mountains have incredible fall colors

77. Christiansburg, VA (New River Gorge National Park and Preserve)

78. Troutville, VA

79. Vesuvius, VA (Mallard Duck Campground; Vesuvius Mountain; Blue Ridge Parkway)—last big climb

80. Greenville, VA (bike shop: Blue Ridge Cyclery, in Charlottesville, VA)

81. Mineral, VA (Haysi Hardware Store)—they gave us hats!

82. Ashland, VA

83. Williamsburg, VA (James River State Park)—the grackles cheered for us

84. Yorktown, VA—The End!

Acknowledgments

I would like to thank my husband, Twain, for his endless support and encouragement—it is astounding. He has been my adventure buddy, my best friend, a loyal father, and my partner for twenty-five years, letting me run my restlessness out and sharing in all my challenges and triumphs. I am so lucky.

I also want to thank my children: Finn, who has always been steady and strong; Jonah, who has opened my eyes to many truths; Raven, who has been patient and comforting; and Oakley, who has given me a reason to never stop trying and to stay strong. They have all put up with my lackadaisical nature and run along beside me on many misguided expeditions.

Thank you also to my family of origin, for letting me be the youngest and being on my side, even when I am getting away with murder.

And to my friends and community who have cheered me on and listened to my endless stories, never once telling me that I was a bore or that I talked too much—you guys are the best.

And lastly, to Michele and Christopher Robbins, Christopher for taking a chance on me and believing that I had a story worth telling and Michele, my editor, who seemed to always know what I was trying to say.

This adventure could have never happened without all the people across the United States that extended kindness to us. Oakley and I were held by strangers who tooted their horns, waved friendly hellos, and offered cool water, a place to sleep, a meal, or their encouragement. These gestures made all the difference to us and fueled us up every hill. It was from them that we learned our greatest lessons.

Author Bio

Leah Day is a licensed clinical social worker living on Peaks Island off the coast of Portland, Maine. Over the last twenty-five years, she has counseled individuals and families in parent support groups; on extended wilderness expeditions for youth at risk; and most recently, in private practice where she works with children, adolescents, and adults struggling with a variety of mental health challenges. She is the mother of four children: two of them are adopted and two are biological.

Her youngest child, Oakley, who biked across America with her from August through October of 2019, has been diagnosed with severe ADHD and a learning disability. She combines her experience in parenting, wilderness leadership, and mental health counseling to give both Oakley and herself a chance to break negative patterns and learn from natural consequences. She has found that adventure, the outdoors, and connecting with others in the community can have life-altering effects on people, and now it is time for her to put these beliefs to the test.

She and Oakley opened Lighthouse Bikes in May of 2021 as a means to continue their adventure together and to share their love of cycling with others. They offer full repair services, bicycle rentals, and tours of the Maine coast.

About Familius

Visit Our Website: www.familius.com

Familius is a global trade publishing company that publishes books and other content to help families be happy. We believe that the family is the fundamental unit of society and that happy families are the foundation of a happy life. We recognize that every family looks different, and we passionately believe in helping all families find greater joy. To that end, we publish books for children and adults that invite families to live the Familius Ten Habits of Happy Family Life: *love together, play together, learn together, work together, talk together, heal together, read together, eat together, give together,* and *laugh together.* Founded in 2012, Familius is located in Sanger, California.

Connect

Facebook: www.facebook.com/familiustalk
Twitter: @familiustalk, @paterfamilius1
Pinterest: www.pinterest.com/familius
Instagram: @familiustalk

The most important work you ever do will be within the walls of your own home.